PREFACF

I have written this book for one reason only and absolutely amazing and courageous mam and to rightfully deserved. To pay homage to her streng throughout her life! In her short years lived on th behind; her story must be told. She was and still is a heroine and what is a story without a hero or a heroine?

She has passed the baton onto me now and there are many reasons why I have written this book, but the main one is to tell you all about a woman who fought her whole life for mostly everyone but herself. A woman who was strong and resolute in her stance against injustice, but the greatest unjust was done when she was not here to make it right.

A woman who was promised the only thing she asked for, a promise not kept. A mother's dying wish. In the short journey I travelled with my mam I gained the necessary tools to continue my life with hope, love and a strong sense of survival.

My life with my mam was filled with much happiness, but hand in hand came a whole lot of heartache. Every word written in this story is from my whole perspective of my life with my mam. These are my memories, and this is my account of what took place.

The words come solely from my heart and soul, and from pure love. I hope whoever reads this book agrees that it had to be a story told and feels the warmth and love of my mother in their hearts also.

She was a true inspiration to me and continues to be so. It has been a hard story to write, resurfacing a lot of feelings that were deeply buried in my heart. I kept them locked away, for me to continue my life in a so-called relatively normal way.

I have learnt much from my life so far; how to be a master of self-preservation has played a huge part in this, taught masterfully to me by the best, my mam.

I am thankful for the person I have become today and have worked hard at it, drawing a lot of my strength from my mam and the wisdom and courage she instilled in me. Without her I would not be the person I am today. I am, and always will be, proud to be her daughter.

Take Care Of The Kids

TERESA COOPER

 and could drink any man under the table, which was
950 's. She would smoke super king after super king
 a good drink. Not the baby Cham for my nanny, she
ed nothing more than to be intoxicated on a frequent

right and read avidly, her literature was exemplary,
faltering vocabulary and grammar. No crossword was
nd she would execute endless puzzles without defeat.
nd engaging, as was her mathematics. She was all in all
ols in the box, but the devil inside had weaved his
the way he made her feel.
like no other I have ever heard in my life. What came
inexplicably obscene. Her most favourite swear word of
believe me she did not say it for the shock factor; well
e may have and then liked the controversy it caused. For a
nt as herself she knew what she wanted and how to behave
path! She was not out to impress anyone. She did what she
e wanted to!
een respectfully taught in a catholic school run by nuns and
to the extreme for her disobedience. She would bite her
ly and was smoking incessantly by the age of nine. Her
deterred pensiveness were to fuel the fire of fury in a strict,
lishment that required ultimate submissiveness.
s a free spirit, and no amount of Hail Mary 's was going to turn
d girl that was expected. It taught her nothing more than
e would act up accordingly. She was not going to be
any religion or anyone! She did not give a damn about the way
ed her and wasn t about to conform for anything or anyone!
uld fuck right off as far as she was concerned!
her tough exterior though was a big heart for the ones she
lly later when we grandkids came along. She was who she was
apologies to anyone, and never would!

became a big sister but by far the stereotypical, conventional
as four years old when her first sister came into the world and
her next little sister made an arrival. She was absolutely besotted
and adored them both; she was also to become extremely
of them, all be it a second mum.
ur of their skin was of no consequence to her, they could have been
en, and it would have made no difference to her at all. They were
, her flesh and blood, and that was all that mattered to her.

ACKNOWLEDGMENTS

I would like to thank my dear husband for supporting me in our time together. For encouraging me to follow my dreams and helping me believe in myself. Oh, and for always making me laugh!

A very special man who has been able to deal with my grief with me and never once judged. I know if it were not for him, I would never have been able to share this story as he has shown me that no matter how hard life gets there is always a reason to get up in the morning.

He is a beacon of light who has been able to lift me out of the darkness without even knowing. He is a beautiful soul, and I will love him until death does us part.

My children for filling me with so much love, I never thought existed. They are my pots of gold at the end of the rainbow, the silver lining in my dark cloud, my diamonds and pearls and treasures so rare, the loves of my life and my eternal saviours. Without them, I would not have had the purpose and pleasure of unconditional love.

They have inspired me to be a better person and taught me to achieve and believe. I am forever theirs and they are the two beings on the entirety of this planet that I owe everything to, for I chose for them to enter my world.

My beautiful brothers and sister, who have all contributed to me being who I am, and have, and in their own ways inspired and motivated me to write this story.

The hardship we have endured together has bound us together for eternity, and even though we have all fought and fell out with each other over the years, we have always been there for one another.

No family can laugh as hard as we do, and no one will ever understand us like we do! I am thankful and blessed to have them all in my life and I will love them all forever.

It was however becoming increasingly apparent that some people did not like or approve of their skin colour, and she learnt about prejudice, hate and racism from an extremely young age. She learnt very quickly how to stand up for the ones she loved!

There was a time she told me that she was bobbing her youngest sister up and down in her pram outside the local butchers, people were passing by and one lad she knew from around where she lived poked his nose into the pram. He started to mimic a monkey.

My mam who had just bought sausages from the butchers whacked them hard over his head. He fell to the ground; she caught him good. She then proceeded to ride the pram backwards and forwards over him whilst he was on the ground. Keeping in mind that back then, those old prams were not lightweight. He squealed in pain to her great satisfaction!

It vilified and angered her that if her mam had other children to a white man, there would of course have been a stigma attached, but not to the extreme she was dealing with. It made her steelier and more protective, to be the best biggest sister there was. Nobody would ever hurt them whilst she had a breath in her body!

My nanny had started spending more time down the pub, so my mam took on the mother role and was a complete natural, but in order to make sure her sisters were looked after she had to skip school! She went to thirteen different schools in Leeds. It was not because she was thick or stupid (as they used to say in them days) it was because she had to be at home for her sisters and that was just the way it was. My mam had already accepted that was just the way it was going to be and for me, that showed a huge amount of integrity for such a young age.

She told me she would put her reddest lipstick on and wear the highest heels and chew gum like she was as common as muck. The head teachers would take one look at her and would have already made their mind up, there was no chance they were having a girl of her deplorable substance tainting their school's image.

Nobody asked questions and nobody wanted to know why this young girl was the way she was. Judgement was high in its moral standing back then and if your face did not fit then no questions were asked!!

My mam though was emotionally of very high intelligence. She knew how to play every fiddle because she had to. Always one step ahead of the game and without any qualifications, she could outsmart the cleverest person with her quick wit and charm.

She was especially close to her youngest sister who looked at my mam as her mother. To a degree, my mam relished in this as her mam was spasmodic in her parental stature and because of this there was nothing my mam did not do for her little sisters.

All be it, it was a huge responsibility for a young girl, and it was bound to have repercussions down the line.

My little baby I will rock you to sleep.

Your mammy I am and you I will keep.

I will bring sunshine to brighten your days.

Whilst you are with me,

You never shall weep.

I know my mams relationship with her mam was fractious, but she could not just stop loving her! She tried her best to understand nanny's life, for hers was another story altogether. My nanny had given up her first born after my grandad had left. It was a boy and he had been adopted by her adoptive parents. They were good people, but for her, it was the hardest decision she had ever had to make.

She could not forgive herself though, and I believe it was one of the reasons which contributed to why she behaved like she did not give a fuck. I think everyone else seemed to be judging her, so she had to make herself bullet proof. I know through conversations that I had with my nanny later on in her life that it was sheer hell for her.

The only reason she chose to keep my mam was because she was so sunny and bright and was a much easier child. My mam would just mould into any circumstance that would arise, effortlessly. Her son on the other hand needed lots of attention and cried pretty much consistently. It still though was a heart-breaking decision.

There were a lot of reasons that made my nanny the complex person she was. More often than not when you scratch away at the surface of the most hardened people, they usually have the saddest past. You never know what a person has experienced to make them the way they are. My mam seemed to understand this about my nanny and my nanny knew this. My nanny became very manipulative with my mam and was A star qualified at it.

Over the years, my mam compensated for the fact she was the child that was kept instead of her brother who had been given away. My nanny's drinking turned her into a Jekyll and Hyde character. Sober she was a doting lovely mam but drunken, her demons would surface, and she would become a petulant and nasty menace, bullying, and ridiculing in order to gain control of anything and anyone she felt she had an advantage over. She was divulging her insecurities and failings all onto my mam!

My mam was walking on eggshells with my nanny on a daily basis and the resentment was building inside of my mam at the same daily rate.

My mam never got to meet her dad, and this troubled her exceptionally. She tried to find him, but the shame that was bestowed on him was so much more than a need to see his child.

My mam had formed her own idealism about life, and this had equipped her to concentrate on the good things and the blessings. She was not a person to dwell on the negative, and fortunately so as her life was not mapped out that way. Nothing or nobody could keep her down. Her spirit was made of fire and her demeanour was proud and strong; for a young lady she was wise and knowledgeable of society 's expectations.

It was a love hate relationship between my mam and my nanny, and my mam would come to despise the drink that had gripped my nanny's tortured soul.

Shame has no mercy on her tortured soul.

She devours the suffering into the entirety of her whole.

The loathing of her choices are sewed deep into her memory.

As the whisky absorbs the quagmire of her misery.

Torment dominates the tranquillity of night,

Opulence and peace are way out of sight.

For all of her penances she will pay,

No rest the for the wicked some might say.

I was born in Leeds in the early 70 's. Both of my parents derived from strong stock and combined they were an ultimate force to be reckoned with. They were both good people and liked to laugh (most of the time). I will always be grateful for their perspectives on life, wisdom, and combined senses of humour.

I was the third child and probably the most difficult to a degree. I loved to scream at the top of my lungs for no apparent reason. My mam would put me in my bedroom, go downstairs and play the radio as loud as she could to drown me out. I was insistent on wanting to be heard and was out to make my mark from the minute I was born. I could not be pacified or subdued in any way and my mam had no experience in this. She was a complete natural with babies and I had come along to show her otherwise. It hurt her pride and she did not like me very much at times because of it (her words).

It turns out I had developed pneumonia. I was nine months old and was severely poorly with it; to the point a priest had to be called to the hospital to initiate the last rights! I was a fighter though and pulled through.

It was not until I could communicate that I eased up on my interminable wailing! By now though my mam had been burdened with guilt and my screaming was nothing in comparison to me not being here at all.

I did not get much easier after that as by all accounts I had an answer for everything. I wanted to know the ins and outs of everything and was always asking questions to things my mam had no knowledge of. I started singing at the same time I could talk and was giving Shirley Bassey a run for her money morning, noon, and night!

My mam would say I had been here before, and I felt like I had. I had a distinct insight about what was to happen next. I learnt much later in life, that this was passed down through my nanny and her gypsy blood.

I was also plagued with extremely bad ear infections. I had perforations to both my ear drums by the time I was two and had to have weekly visits to the hospital for the next seven years of my life! Now I realise that in a lot of ways my mam was quite soft with me and nearly losing me must have been the reason why.

Things became so much more bearable for my mam when I finally started school! I absolutely loved school and it was what I needed. My mind was a sponge and I found everything easy. I particularly remember one occasion after talking about birds in my new class, when the teacher asked if anyone knew what migration meant.

My hand flew in the air, and I can still recollect the look of bemusement on her face as if to say, "Here we go." I stated it was when a bird must go to another country to get food to survive the cold. She then asked me if I knew of a bird that did this. "A Swallow," I replied. It was my first term at school, I was five years old. The teacher called my parents into the school, and it was agreed they could evaluate me on my academic abilities. I was nearly three years above my age on everything.

My mam and dad were not shocked in any way. I was their child and both of them knew my abilities. My dad more so than anyone loved this because he was very academic, but his life had lured him into murky waters and what he did not know at the time was just how hard he would have to swim to survive.

My dad worked away on the oil rigs so he would be away for long periods of time. My mam got caught pregnant with my younger brother pretty much straight after me, and he came along one year and three weeks later. She had four children in the space of five years. We were undoubtedly a formidable force.

We lived on one of the roughest council estates in Leeds at the time and were taught to stand up for ourselves. My dad was an ex-boxer, an Irish catholic from Belfast, and knew how hard life could be. He inevitably passed on his skills to us, and I remember vividly at the age of two being taught how to give a punch and to duck and dive as to not receive one.
We were tough and were taught how to fight!

There was the four us. Big brother, big sister, me and the baby brother.
My big brother was my saviour growing up. He was so protective of me and for that he will always hold a special place in my heart. He had seen an awful lot more than I did, and understood a lot more than I did. He was the one that when I got scared at the late-night arguments would always let me get into the bottom of his bed.
 I felt lucky to have him. He shielded me from a lot and made my life easier. He was wise beyond his years and was always kind to me. He had the possession of equilibrium from the day he was born. He was very special and even though he may have teased me from time to time, the minute I became upset he would stop. He did not have a vindictive, nasty streak in the whole of his body. Well, that is how I seen him, but I was under no illusion, that it was not how everyone perceived him to be.
 My sister was two and a half years older than me and was not a girl to cross in anyway. You messed with her and that would be at your own peril. She would match anyone like for like and if you wanted to play dirty then rest assured, she would play dirtier. It was clear from a young age that she would stop at nothing to win.
 My younger brother was the 'baby' and we all treated him accordingly. He could never do any wrong in my mams eyes and used it to his full advantage to say the least. We were best friends and the worst of enemies at times, but I was extremely protective of him and that would last a lifetime.

My mam was her own unique entity. She was an enigmatic and enchanting woman, who beguiled all who would ever meet her. She got on with whatever she had to, however she had to. She had the highest morals and expected the same from all around her, she was kind and empathetically considerate to everyone, but she did not suffer fools gladly. She could not abide small mindedness and would not engage in gossip with the likes of so. She called a spade a spade and exuded truth.

My mam did not need anyone and if she chose a friend then she chose well and she was the loyalist friend they would ever have. Her best friend was a lovely, warm and charismatic soul. Whom also, luckily for me, also had a daughter, the same age as me. My best friend for life.

My mam in essence, did what she had to do, and let everybody else do what they had to do. She was a busy person moving forward in her life, and had her mind set on her future. Our house was always kept immaculate, the best on the street without a doubt. My mam liked her home to be clean. Spic and Span.

At the time of us being young, brass was the desired effect and every one of her ornaments was polished to oblivion. You would never see any brass anywhere as shinier as my mams. She did this for her own satisfaction only as she was never in competition with nobody, she did not need to be, and I believe she found it therapeutic.

She was only five foot tall, but you would never have thought so. She had an immense strength of character and was a straight talker. She could make someone feel like the greatest person on the planet but one of her dirty looks could have cut you in half. Her overall persona was warm and sunny, and she had charisma in abundance.

She stood no nonsense from anyone. Big, tall, short, black, white or whoever the person may have been, if she were in the right she would never back down. Like she used to say to us all 'Even if you are shaking in your boots, if you are right, you are never to back down!"

Till this day I still apply this to myself!

Nobody really got on my mams wrong side because above all, people respected her honesty and integrity, and most people wanted to be liked by her. She was a good energy who people wanted to be around. She made people feel safe and her sense of humour was incredibly magnetic.

She overall just loved to laugh!

Love is held at its lowest at times.

Its worth though exceeds all fortunes and gold.

Behold love though,

For it is the epitome of all that should be treasured.

And we possess right there, within our hold.

TWO

MY DAD

My dad was born in Belfast, Falls Road to be exact, in 1943. He was an exceedingly, clever man and he found education and learning to be effortless. After leaving school it was hard for him to secure a job, mainly because he was a catholic and he was persecuted for this, so he told me.

He had had enough of the divide between the Catholics and Protestants and by the age of fifteen had been embroiled in too many protests and riots, with scars all over his face to prove it!

His mother put religion over the love of her children and was extremely cold and detached because of it. My dad and his brother were taught by the Irish Christian Brothers in their younger days and were vilified and subjected to bad beatings for the most trivial reasons. I learnt later on down the line; his brother had worse things done to him.

How terribly sad and demoralising, that an establishment ran by a religion would inflict such atrocities on young children in the name of a God.

My dad was a deep soul and did not talk for the sake of conversation. Anything he had to say was deliberate and meaningful, he was a brooder and a philanthropist at heart, but the cruel misgivings of his childhood had made him steely and untrusting towards people and their intentions.

He had inherited a stammer in his time with the Irish Christian brothers and was deeply embarrassed about the profound effect it had on his speech. He could sing prolifically any song though and would sing day and night if he could of. He became masterful over his stammer and very few people would have known he had it. He was a tremendously proud man and exuded confidence in plentitude.

His ma, for one, had taught him that he was beneath her expectations and wanted him to embrace the catholic religion above everything he knew. As far as she was concerned, he was disrespectful and did not appreciate his education.

She could not have cared less how he was being treated, but she would relish in telling her astute, orthodox circle of acquaintances of how he was being taught by the Irish Christian Brothers and how boastful about it she was!

His ma, my grandma, was not short of a bob or two. She was a meticulous seamstress and was well in demand for her expertise and exquisite detail. I was told she had a few franchises and was quite the businesswoman (whether this is true or not, I don't actually know). She was though, very shrewd, and stingy!

He told me that one time he needed some money for something or another and his ma had told him she did not have any. He must have been desperate to ask her in the first place. Unbeknown to her, she did not realise he knew where she kept her secret stash. It was at the top of the stairs, hidden underneath her precious statue of the Virgin Mary.

He took the money he needed and started jumping up and down and shouting at the top of his voice "Ma there has been a miracle; our lady has just provided me with the money I had been praying for." My grandma's face apparently turned white. He kissed her on her cheek whilst skipping out the house rejoicing in miracles.

She never said anything to him, what could she say. She was a mean, spirited woman. My dad's charm and cleverness must have cut her to the core. This story still makes me laugh today. There is always more than one way to skin a cat.

This tale encapsulated him completely!

My dad left Ireland at the age of fifteen to join the merchant navy as a way out. Two years later, he went back to Belfast and stole his brother away to join him. His younger brother in my dad's time at sea, had become involved with a certain Irish rebellion group. It was something to do with counterfeit money.

This particular night, whilst his brother was sleeping, he awoke to a gun being pointed at his head. It was mistaken identity, but his brother's hair with the shock had literally turned white overnight. It was too much for my dad to bear; he had to get him away.

My uncle was easily led, and always seemed to be getting himself involved in some commotion or another. My dad had to keep a firm grip on him. They were like chalk and cheese, but their despondent pasts were to become their unequivocal bind for life.

Leeds became their choice of destination where a lot of the Irish tended to settle back then in the sixties. Leeds was an aspiring city, offering prosperous work opportunities. My dad had the work ethic and grafted hard. This was

new beginnings for him, and he was grasping the good times that Ireland could not give him.

My dad in a way, was a replica of my nanny. He did not give a flying fuck who liked him or did not. He was a man who had been through extreme hardship but wore it well. He was exceptionally confident and a superlatively, attractive man. Short, smart, and handsome! There was no hang up 's in being the five foot, five inches of the man he was. He was big and mighty in his stature and could hold his own with ease.

His mentality was impermeable. He was mindfully strong!

If two worlds collided it was the day that he and my mam met! My dad was seven years older than her and was not out to impress her in any other way than being who he was. My mam was captivated at once. He had seen the world and possessed charm and maturity like my mam had never known. My mam was way older than her years and was ready to start a family of her own. My dad ticked all the right boxes, and she was smitten.

My dad liked a drink and at the time my mam seen this as part of his charm. My nanny told me that when my mam invited him over to meet her and her sisters for the first time, they heard a man singing in the distance at the top of his voice. He must have been at least two streets away. He was singing of a sweet love he had met and a love he was going to keep! It was my dear dad, and he was half cut! My mam was embarrassed to high heaven.

My nanny however, had already endeared him to her. She liked him, and nanny didn't like anyone!! They both enjoyed a drink or two and whilst my mam was not at all teetotal, she could take it or leave it.

My nanny and my dad had similar things happen to them and could identify with each other. All authority had shown the two of them was of power endowed egos. They were sympathisers of one another, and their bond was instant. My dad had nothing to hide, but he would only ever let the people that mattered know his true soul.

It was not long before my mam became pregnant with my big brother and that was that. She was 19. By all accounts he was a gorgeous baby with the biggest, bluest eyes. This seemed to cause quite a lot of speculation and controversy, considering my dad was dark and had dark brown eyes!

People talked, especially on an estate where everyone assumed they knew everyone else 's business! My dad knew otherwise and told me years later he never doubted that my brother was not his and loved him immediately.

Still, my dad liked his freedom! Not in the play the field type of way, he liked being a free spirt and decided to go off to sea once again. He came back, my sister was conceived and then off he went again. By this time, my mam had delivered him an ultimatum! Stay or leave.

He chose to stay. I came along two and half years after my sister, followed by my partner in crime (my little brother) one year and three weeks later.

My dad worked hard and earned good money which pleased my mam as she liked nice things. For someone who came from nothing she had an eye for style and had acquired an expensive taste for fancy décor and fine materials. She liked antiques and knew quality when she seen it. Her standards were high in every possible way.

My dad kept her pacified within these realms and he laboured hard to ensure she was indulged. He would come back from his stints of working away throwing money in the air and all us kids would scramble for it! It was only coppers, but it entertained us to no end.

He was a softy really, and I knew it. I got him completely. I was a daddy's girl, and he was the center of my world!

He did though have a much darker side which more than often was evoked by the dreaded drink. He could turn in an instant and could be very menacing and intimidating when he chose to be.

One particular time he was refused a drink in a pub he frequented; the last orders had been called. He had been served numerous times beforehand, but new management had taken over and were putting their foot down! He made it clear he was not happy and left the pub festering.

The next day he returned to the pub and at last orders he ordered a round of drinks for the whole of the pub. He was applauded and thanked profusely, for after all it was an extremely generous gesture, and he raised his glass for a toast, with everyone that was there.

When he was asked to pay, he told the new management that he would not be paying for the drinks, and that the management would put them on the house. They did not argue with my dad, and he was never refused a drink again.

He would fight anyone of any size and relished in the fact 'The bigger they are, the harder they fall." He would boast this, and he did not need any Dutch courage (alcohol) to enable him to do so. In actual fact, to some degree, I think a few drinks softened his intent.

We were having a family day out and on this particular day we were going to a top family resort. We arrived full of excitement and joy but as my dad went to park his car another car nicked his place. He had been indicating for the space and it was obvious my dad was going to use it, and this infuriated him! Whenever he got angry, he would become quiet and detached. He would never shout an expletive, that was not his style. It was all about actions for him. He proceeded to walk over to the car and explained to the man driving, the factors of what had occurred. My mam was trying to distract us, but we were all mesmerised.

My dad came back to the car and explained to my mam that 'the twat" would be moving. He sat tapping his fingers whilst the man reversed out. He did not give my dad any eye contact at all. My dad made his way into the space and in an instant, he had rectified his mood back to happy dad!

I heard years later that he had threatened the man in front of his wife and family in a way that had terrified the man. If that man did not do as my dad had asked, my dad would have stalked him and his family for the entire day and in the process, he would have dismantled their car!

The thing is my dad would always back up his intentions and most men seen this in him. He had a nasty streak for those who did not comply or adhere to his expectations or who did not want to follow his moral code!

In a way he was notorious and used it to his full advantage. He was not well liked by a lot of people because of his dark side but it never phased him, he did not after all give a flying fuck what anybody thought of him. That in itself unsettled people. Most people like being liked, but not my dad and nobody was going to make a fool out of him in any way at all. Well, not without paying for it, and most people did not want the bother.

He would do what he wanted and for the size of him it was unbelievable. He had connections too and news travels very fast. Whether it be in a small town or a big city, word soon gets around. He was not to be upset!

Having said that though, he was not sadistic and was not a bully. He generally would have had to have been provoked in some way. If he thought any injustice had been done to him, he would not and could not let it lie. I think a lot of people avoided him like the plague.

He had an unquenched thirst for the bookies also. He loved to bet on the horses and would blow money like the wind. Every so often he would have a huge win and would splash out on everyone and everything. We always had a decent car and nice clothes, and were lucky to be able to holiday for a week here and there in England. Devon and North Yorkshire. We had days out at all the big family resorts.

He was always generous and when the good times rolled, we were winning at life, but I also to dread to think about the money he wasted whilst chasing his millionaire 's dream.

This was to be his Achilles heel!

He on occasion would turn up after a night out with some animal he had bought from down the pub. We kids would be ecstatic, but my mam would hit the roof.

One time it was a tortoise who managed to escape!!! Then a dog that was so wild it had to be kept on a long leash at all times in the back garden. You could not pet it as it would have had your hand off.

All in all, he was thinking of us kids, but his choices were of a man who had quite clearly drank beyond his clarity of judgement. I mean, I always questioned how that dog never had my dad for its dinner!

It was only the good side I got to see of my dad. He could not do any wrong in my eyes whatsoever. His whole demeanour made me feel safe and secure and he instilled his unwavering confidence in me.

I hung off his every word and he knew this, I could do no wrong his eyes, much to the annoyance of my mam.

I was a daddy's girl through and through!

A child becomes a man,

Before the child has time to be,

Injustice is so burdensome;

No eye can ever see.

Ingrained so deeply into his soul.

Etched fiercely into his pride.

The suffering caused by others,

Simmering away inside.

There is no time to sit and wonder,

There is no time to grieve.

The consequences festering,

With illimitable reprieve.

ACKNOWLEDGMENTS

I would like to thank my dear husband for supporting me in our time together. For encouraging me to follow my dreams and helping me believe in myself. Oh, and for always making me laugh!

A very special man who has been able to deal with my grief with me and never once judged. I know if it were not for him, I would never have been able to share this story as he has shown me that no matter how hard life gets there is always a reason to get up in the morning.

He is a beacon of light who has been able to lift me out of the darkness without even knowing. He is a beautiful soul, and I will love him until death does us part.

My children for filling me with so much love, I never thought existed. They are my pots of gold at the end of the rainbow, the silver lining in my dark cloud, my diamonds and pearls and treasures so rare, the loves of my life and my eternal saviours. Without them, I would not have had the purpose and pleasure of unconditional love.

They have inspired me to be a better person and taught me to achieve and believe. I am forever theirs and they are the two beings on the entirety of this planet that I owe everything to, for I chose for them to enter my world.

My beautiful brothers and sister, who have all contributed to me being who I am, and have, and in their own ways inspired and motivated me to write this story.

The hardship we have endured together has bound us together for eternity, and even though we have all fought and fell out with each other over the years, we have always been there for one another.

No family can laugh as hard as we do, and no one will ever understand us like we do! I am thankful and blessed to have them all in my life and I will love them all forever.

ONE

MY MAM HER MAM AND ME

A mother is our first love. A mother is like no other for she has held us in her womb and encumbered us to her soul. A mother is a slave to our calling as we are the gluttony of her whole. A mother is love who expects nothing in return.

My mother was an angel.

The day I lost my mother will never leave me. I was 15 years old. She had been ill for about a year. She was the strongest woman I have ever known and until this day no other woman has shown me, not even half of her courage or strength.

My mam was born in 1950. She was the second child to be born to my nanny and my grandad (whom I never met). Their marriage ended after my nanny had an affair with a Black man, she had met him down the local pub and I knew him to be my grandad. My nanny became pregnant and when my aunty was born, she was of obvious mixed race.

My nannies husband up and absconded without a word of acknowledgment to my nanny. He had been ridiculed and was ultimately scorned; his pride had been immeasurably dented. My nanny had made the biggest fool out of him and not just with a white man, but with a Jamaican immigrant! The shame was colossal for a man of his substance. He was a hardworking, conformist and a traditionalist of all men, who expected his wife to honour and obey him.

How he thought my nanny could adhere to this was unfathomable as she could never in a million years be the dutiful wife who was expected; she had a thirst for excitement, and some may have said the devil resided in her. She was a wild, free spirit who had been suppressed her whole life and by trying to tame her, had resulted in her unleashing her insatiable defiance.

My nanny was an actual Romany gypsy who was adopted as a child, but the gypsy was very much still in her, and she subsequently defied any so-called normality '.

Naturally beautiful, she could have had any man she desired. She did what she wanted when she wanted, and her freedom was substantially her essence

1

in life. She loved the pub and could drink any man under the table, which was quite unheard of in the 1950's. She would smoke super king after super king and hand in hand went a good drink. Not the baby Cham for my nanny, she liked the whisky and liked nothing more than to be intoxicated on a frequent basis.

She was extremely bright and read avidly, her literature was exemplary, which matched her unfaltering vocabulary and grammar. No crossword was ever left unfinished, and she would execute endless puzzles without defeat. Her mind was sharp and engaging, as was her mathematics. She was all in all one of the sharpest tools in the box, but the devil inside had weaved his magic, and she liked the way he made her feel.

Her language was like no other I have ever heard in my life. What came from her mouth was inexplicably obscene. Her most favourite swear word of all was 'cunt" and believe me she did not say it for the shock factor; well perhaps initially she may have and then liked the controversy it caused. For a woman as intelligent as herself she knew what she wanted and how to behave and she chose her path! She was not out to impress anyone. She did what she wanted because she wanted to!

My nanny had been respectfully taught in a catholic school run by nuns and she was punished to the extreme for her disobedience. She would bite her nails compulsively and was smoking incessantly by the age of nine. Her resilience and undeterred pensiveness were to fuel the fire of fury in a strict, conformed establishment that required ultimate submissiveness.

My nanny was a free spirit, and no amount of Hail Mary's was going to turn her into the good girl that was expected. It taught her nothing more than defiance and she would act up accordingly. She was not going to be suppressed by any religion or anyone! She did not give a damn about the way society regarded her and wasn't about to conform for anything or anyone! Everybody could fuck right off as far as she was concerned!

Underneath her tough exterior though was a big heart for the ones she loved, especially later when we grandkids came along. She was who she was and made no apologies to anyone, and never would!

So, my mam became a big sister but by far the stereotypical, conventional type. She was four years old when her first sister came into the world and seven when her next little sister made an arrival. She was absolutely besotted with them and adored them both; she was also to become extremely protective of them, all be it a second mum.

The colour of their skin was of no consequence to her, they could have been bright green, and it would have made no difference to her at all. They were her sisters, her flesh and blood, and that was all that mattered to her.

THREE

COUNCIL LIFE

Our house was a small, three bedroom semi-detached with a good-sized back garden and a fair size front garden with room to park our Brown Cortina Estate, which my dad prided himself on. My brothers shared a room, as did my sister and me.

My sister would always get to pick where she had her bed first, as she was the oldest and that was just the way it was. We would both have preferred to have our own rooms, as quite frankly we did not get along.

Two and half years is quite an age difference when you are young, and my sister always seemed so much older than me. She made no bones about letting me know that I annoyed the hell out of her, so I just tried to stay out of her way, and it seemed to work okay for most of the time.

Our estate was rough. There were a lot of characters. Some good, some bad, but I was a savvy kid and had been taught to differentiate between the two. I had also been taught to use my instinct and gut intuition. Something I have taught my children to do so also, it is a necessity in life and a life skill, that is probably the thing I have relied on more in my life than anything else. I also believe that the fact there was only a difference of five years between the four of us siblings helped immensely as I was never usually alone.

I was a tomboy, no doubt about it. I would ride my bike, which did not have brakes, from the top of the hill to the bottom. More often than not, I would end up flying off and scabbing my knees, which as gross as it was, they were nearly always septic.

I absolutely loved the thrill of danger. I had roller skates which my brother oiled that were fast as lighting. I prided myself on being the best at everything and I must have literally irritated the hell out of everyone because of it!

I would make mud pies, play marbles in the mud, collect worms and caterpillars, climb trees, jump off shed roofs, race the boys, and fight the boys! I was not scared of anything or anyone. I was always out playing; we all were back then. We were not allowed to get under our mam's feet and as long as it was dry, we would be out from morning until teatime. We would only know it was teatime because mam would shout mine, my sister and brothers names in order of age at the top of her voice. We would all drop what we were doing at once and run in for tea.

My mam was quite the cook (she had had years of experience), and we generally always had a pudding. She prided herself on us all being well fed. You did not have snacks back then so you would be ravenous and grateful (well most times) and if you were not grateful, you didn t get a second choice. You couldn t leave your main meal as you wouldn t have your pudding! I particularly detested liver and onions.

On one occasion, she had cooked this for tea and treacle pudding was for dessert. It was to be a dilemma and an ordeal for me both at the same time. I sat for what felt like an eternity, forcing the liver down so to have the treacle pudding. It was also getting dark outside, and I was missing out on valuable play time.

I remember feeling like my mam was torturing me and thinking about how unfair and nasty she was, but I ate it, and the treacle pudding was so scrumptious that I forgave her.

In hindsight, it taught me a very valuable lesson! To be thankful and to count my blessings, that being, that my mam ensured the best for us.

The house conjoining ours had the most beautiful garden I had ever seen, and the roses were the most colourful and exquisite I had ever seen. I was truly captivated by them and decided I was going to pick a load of them, some to make perfume with and the rest to keep in my bedroom to make it look pretty. I did not think for a minute this was a naughty thing to do, I just thought they were so special, and I had to have them! I was in my element until the neighbour came knocking at the door.

My mam was not happy at all, and she sat me down at the kitchen table under the pretence she had telephoned the police. I realised then the enormity of my actions and sat there crying my little eyes out. I wrote a letter of apology to the neighbour and delivered it personally. They were in fact very kind about the whole ordeal after they realised my actions were not out of malice but of sheer innocence. They had spent years pruning and making their little garden their sanctuary, and I had all but butchered it!

I was not a vandal though, just very naive. I never picked another flower from anyone s garden again and even though my mams punishment seemed extreme toward a five-year-old, she taught me well. Of course, she never phoned the police, but I had to be made aware that every action has a consequence. It would be very much debated nowadays but back then if you did wrong, you were made to pay for it, and it did not do any of us any harm!

We lived a little way from some train tracks, and we would spend hours down there playing chicken (where you hear a train coming and run over the tracks) so not to get hit by the train! I must have only been about five or six! We would play knock on ginger (where you would knock on someone's door then leg it)!

We were always up to some sort of mischief!

There was a big hill right at the bottom of our street which was named the black hills and one day I was on my own and walked to the top of this hill. There was no one about and I just stood admiring the most scenic view. I was quite in my element as I loved nature and was captivated by the sheer beauty of everything my eyes were beholding.

Suddenly, I heard a rustle from some bushes nearby and became instinctively on my guard. Out popped a man who I had never seen before. He had a long coat and was tall. He had a messy beard and looked dirty and unkempt. He asked me if I was lost and if he could help me? He told me I was the prettiest little girl he had ever seen, and would I like to go on a little walk with him?

I knew instantly he was a bad man and immediately my gut instinct kicked in. I started shouting and screaming at the top of my voice that he was a fucking pervert "Pervert a fucking pervert. There's a PERVERT HELLLLLP, HELLLP MEEEEE" I can tell you that a Banshee had nothing on me, and it worked as intended, he ran for his life.

Now, my mam and dad would never condone swearing from any of us at all, but my dad said that if I ever felt that I needed to get out of that type of situation then I could swear at the top of my voice and scream at the top of my lungs. I surely did both of those things right there and then! The man looked bewildered for a second, then just turned on his heel and fled.

That man must have thought it was his lucky day when he seen me wandering along. He must have had the shock of his life when my mouth opened and out popped that shrill, booming shriek! Hopefully, it may have deterred him or even prevented him in the future!

I ran as fast as my little legs could carry me to my house, in through the front door, like a shot. The words were spewing out of my mouth, with no time to stop and catch my breath. My knees were knocking, and my hands were shaking.

My dad was ultimately proud of me, but I could see the mist descend over his eyes whilst he pulled his boots on and whilst my mam cuddled me, my dad flew out the house and was up those black hills as fast as lightning.

He was gone a while, but it was fruitless, the dirty man had well and truly disappeared and luckily for him he had. I swear if my dad had caught him, he would have killed him, and I one hundred percent believe this. I never went up those black hills on my own ever again.

By this time, I had started at the local catholic primary school. Nuns and teachers partly ran it. It was a lovely catholic school with a decent reputation and my mam was as proud as punch. My younger brother and I attended the primary school, whilst my sister and eldest brother attended the middle school which was directly adjacent to ours.

I was probably any teachers dream. I was studious and extremely clever. I was reading books way beyond my years, and I found everything easy. I was polite and considerate, and no bully would have dared to take me on as I also had the advantage of being quite handy with my little fists and I was not afraid of using them if ever necessary!

My youngest brother was a real mammy's boy and hated school, my mam mollycoddled him as he was the baby, and all he wanted was to be at home with her. He did not have my academic ability, but of course he was clever in other ways.

One occasion has always been embedded in my mind where he had gone into school as usual, and he must have been chastised by one of the nuns. He went full throttle on her and shouted to her that she had a "buggy fanny"!!

It transpires that my eldest brother had given him a lesson on what the nuns were all about. He'd probably been told off by one perhaps. He didn't have a good view of them it seemed. I can only imagine he advised my younger brother to yell that at them if they were nasty to him. My younger brother wasn't that naive to know it wasn't naughty and he obviously didn't need telling twice!

My mam and dad were called in to the school of course and whilst the school were up in arms at the sheer atrocity, my dad found the whole incident utterly hilarious! My mam and dad went to school and played the embarrassed and equally mortified parents, but both of them were putting on the dutiful act.

He came very close to being expelled but my parent's charm and charisma managed to win the day! Both of my brothers however, were given a talking too, but that was it! "Kids are kids" my dad would say, we were allowed to make mistakes.

We went on holiday for a week to North Yorkshire and stayed in a caravan. We had a ball like you are supposed to whilst on holiday, but by the end of it we were all looking forward to going home! We arrived back to an empty house. We had been burgled!

My dad did not involve the police; it was not the done thing where we lived. Most people managed it by themselves, the police were scum as far as my dad was concerned, they were all corrupt and he hated authority. Nobody in authority had ever helped him and it was fiercely emblazoned in his mind. He would sort it in his own way, and he would accost them accordingly. He knew how to sniff out a rat and he was exceptionally mastered at the craft!

He put the feelers out. He knew a lot of people and would not rest until he found out who had done it. Within a matter of days, he soon did!

It turned out it was someone my dad knew from down the pub. I am not sure quite what happened, but I know the man would have been given the beating of his life and I was told that he and his family had moved away shortly after!

There was a house up the road that had been set on fire! There were druggies living up that road too. That road was off bounds completely. If we were to ever get caught up there, our fingers would have been put in the fire. (They would not have been, but the threat had to ensure that we did not). I realised a few years later there was a paedophile living up there also. It really was a complete dumping ground for the lowest of the low.

Amongst everything that was going on, one of us would almost certainly be fighting someone, mostly my sister! You crossed her and you would regret it! There was a girl in the street who had done just that, and my sister absolutely pummeled the crap out of her. What made my sister more dangerous than all of us though, was that she did not have a cut-off point, she would literally just black out.

This particular incident was beyond scary. All the kids in the street were circling the fight, chorusing 'fight, fight, fight, fight," but instinctively we all knew it had gone way too far. Someone had to run and get an adult and they had to pull my sister off whilst she seemed to be in a trance like state. It was a bizarre thing to witness, and I have to say, it unsettled me. The girl was taken to hospital and her parents called the police.

My sister must have been seven years old at the time. I know my mam was worried, but my dad seemed to disconnect himself from the whole thing. It was not dealt with accordingly. The lack of attachment towards my sister was obvious and my dad was just not interested in her at all.

Looking back now, I believe the religious element of his upbringing brought my dad to certain conclusions about people. In his mind he had decided that the devil had some sort of hold over her, when in actual fact she was crying out for attention from him.

He relished in the fact he had taught us to stand up for ourselves and we believed it made him proud of us. Instead of taking that time with my sister to explain she had gone too far, he had already made his mind up that she was a wrong one. Without even saying those words that is exactly how he made her feel. She was seven years old! He made her feel utterly worthless, whilst making me feel like I was a queen.

None of us would take any messing and the minute the adrenaline kicked in, we would just fight. We would never have run; it would not have been worth the wrath at home.

There was a large family that lived down the bottom of our street. They were nice kids but were avoided by pretty much all the kids on the estate. They were dirty, smelly and unkempt. Their house looked like a tip on the outside and when one of the girls invited me in, I would always decline. I dreaded to think what their house looked like on the inside and above all their dad gave me the eegie beegies.

Looking back now, I realise that those kids were terribly neglected and most probably being abused. They would never have been nasty to anyone and were just desperate for friendship. I often wondered what happened to those kids.

It was on a trip over to my aunties on the day that the dog came into our lives. We were over visiting my auntie's new house and I could not tell you what had happened, but I had been told off for something and I was sat at the bottom of the stairs sulking. The front door was open and in walked the most handsome dog I had ever seen. He was black with tan dots above his eyes and tan paws. He just walked straight over to me wagging his tail.
It was love at first sight!

I was crying, hugging him, and telling him how much I hated my mam for telling me off! He just sat there until I finished.

By this time, I had decided in my little mind that I wanted to keep him and had forgiven my mam, so I went into the kitchen to ask her, whilst the dog followed me behind.

My mam was having none of it to begin with, but I was persistent. In the end she said I could keep him but only if he followed me to the bus stop. I really think she thought there was no chance, that he had a home and would just go home. He did not though.

He followed me all the way to the bus stop and jumped on the bus. Then proceeded to jump on the next bus and then followed us all the way home and he never left!

I mean looking back, why did I just presume he was mine and I was entitled to him? I really believe he was sent to me that dog. I just loved him. In effect though, we did steal him, but by his own free will!

He was no bother to anyone. He walked himself and made friends with the local butcher, so he was always fed. All he wanted was a warm bed at night. That dog had more sophistication and charm than most humans I knew. He was cool and when they say dogs look like their owners, well he really did!

He was a bugger though. I had a budgie at the time and one morning I had gone downstairs as usual but noticed the budgie sitting stiff on his perch. He had died and I was devastated.

My mam let me give him a burial in our back garden to soften the blow; I made him a cross out of two ice lolly sticks and dug a hole. I attentively buried him whilst giving a rendition of the Lord 's Prayer. My mam held my hand and patted it for reassurance, and I felt I had done my little budgie justice.

A little while later I heard a commotion out the front of the house. Loads of people were gathered and laughing their heads off. I ran out to witness the dog running down the ginnel (which was adjacent to our house) with the budgie hanging out of his mouth!

He had dug it up (which was not hard) and decided he was having it! He would go for gerbils and any other animal that I ever owned too, but he would never even growl at a kid.

When the ice-cream van would come to our street, blaring its music out, the dog would sit out the front of the house, howling like a wolf. He proceeded to do for the entirety of his life, every time he heard an ice cream van. My mam decided because of this, that his previous owners must have owned an ice-cream van!!

His speciality, above all was to chase after cars. He would be behind the back wheel, running and barking like a complete lunatic. The dog was just nuts, in the best possible way!

My youngest brother and I would always share a bath on a Sunday and a Wednesday. On one occasion we had a fight and ended up grabbing each other 's hair and pulling each other under the water. Neither of us were going to give in, and if it were not for our dad realising it had gone deathly quiet, then I dread to think how it would have ended. My dad raced in the bathroom and shouted for my mam. It took both of them to free our hands and detangle them from each other 's hair!

We would play pretend houses where we had an imaginary kitchen, living room, bedroom, and garage etc. It would play out lovely until one of us (generally him) parked the car in the imaginary kitchen, instead of the imaginary garage, then all hell would break loose.

We wanted to maim each other so bad over the most trivial of things, but the intent was purposeful, and it was to severely hurt one another. On one of our arguments, he chucked a toy car at me, but it landed in my skull (it had wings). I had to have stitches to close the wound.

As quickly as we fell out though, we would be as quick to make up because it was always way more fun being friends. There was just a very fine line between. We would play up the babysitter to no end. We would sit at the top of the stairs and sing as loudly as we could as to aggravate them. When they would tell us to keep it down, that would be our cue to raise it up a notch.

We were what you called 'little shits'!! Almost feral really!

One of the neighbours at the top of the parade had a huge garden and all the kids would congregate there and play games and dares and so on. Some of the older kids would put so called trances on the other kids whilst chanting 'Concentrate on a piece of white paper," they would then get them to do ridiculous things like strip off or roll in the nettles, and any other stupid stuff really. The thing is, these kids were never actually in a trance but were so daft they would just go along with it, much to everyone else 's amusement.

Ghost stories and weird and wonderful tales were told and there would always be the clown who would go that extra length for the laughs of others.

There were water fights, British bulldog, tag, rounders, football, and lots of other games going on all the time. It was fun and exhilarating to say the least as there were a lot of naughty things going on that our parents would have killed us for (or so we thought) if they had ever have found out.

Most of the time it was good; nothing bad ever happened to me or my younger brother as we had my older brother and sister to look out for us. Everyone knew instinctively to leave us all alone as they would have always come out worse off.

Another neighbour kept a few animals, a cockerel being one. Literally every morning you would hear another neighbour shout out to shut the fucking thing up. There was always some dog barking or some person shouting, but that was just how it was.

I just always remember being happy, content and completely carefree. There was always something happening in our house or on the street, and even though that estate was rough, it was to give me some of the best memories of my life.

My dad was not happy on the estate though and he had had enough, especially since the burglary. He was sick to death of some of the low life scum, and he wanted bigger and better things for his family!

My dad always wanted better in life and he worked extremely hard to earn the money. 'This place is just the first brick" he would say. He had big dreams and aspirations.

Also, even though I never saw my mam cry, worry or fret over things, it didn't mean to say she didn't, she just shielded those things from us from us. My dad would not have liked that in the slightest.

He was a man on a mission!

A light shone amongst us all,

We are no better than our own conscience, are we not?

Our own consequences of our minds,

Our assumptions of the requiems and dreams,

Of what was left behind.

We will continue to enhance our search,

Always hoping to find.

The fortunes and the glory,

Of what is promised to mankind.

FOUR

A NEW START

Things were on the up and we could all feel it! My dad took us to see a house one day. I remember it like yesterday. It was a lot bigger than our three bedroomed semi council house!! I was stood in one of the bedrooms and my dad came in and asked if I liked it. It seemed an odd thing to ask as I was still unsure as to why we were even there.

As it happens, I did like it and that was a great thing to my dad as he had sealed a mortgage and this was going to be my new bedroom! My own bedroom. I was absolutely ecstatic. I had been sharing with my sister and now I would have my own.

The house comprised of four bedrooms. A front room, a dining room and a separate kitchen. The bathroom was upstairs and was massive in comparison to our council one. My bedroom was on the floor with my mam and dad. The attic was converted into two rooms. One which my brothers shared, and my sister had her own like me!

It was more an upmarket part of Leeds, and I was going to start a new school. New beginnings. Pastures new! I was absolutely loving the vibe of life! I never once felt afraid, anxious, or worried about moving, in fact it did not even cross my mind to feel those things. I was just so excited about having my own room, and even though I was only young I sensed this was going to be a much better way of life.

We settled in pretty quickly, as did the dog. There were some shops at the bottom of our street and a butchers happened to be one of them. He would sit and wait outside until the butcher would throw him a few scraps of whatever meat he had lying round. He did not like to be kept waiting either, and on the odd occasion he would run in and help himself. He would often be seen running around the streets with a string of sausages (obviously his favourite) trailing from his mouth.

No one could ever catch him though, he was way too smart, and he knew all the nooks, crannies, and little hideouts. He had it all sussed and sorted! Every now and then someone would come and knock on the door and tell us the butcher was chasing him, with a carving knife in his hand. I remember as clear as day my dad telling them 'Oh he ll be alright, he ll be grand," followed by his dry, deadpan, sardonic laughter. People soon stopped knocking.

I made friends in the street immediately. We all did. School was the same. I was extremely bright and had been noticed for my singing talent. I was starting to stand out, which my mam and dad loved! I had started guitar lessons and was excelling in it, anything musical I just loved, and I would sing to anyone, anytime. I was a natural born performer and was never happier than when I was belting out a song. It drove my mam mad, and she would say "If you are not talking, you are singing." She loved it really.

At least I think she did!

It was whilst living in this house that I would meet my dad's ma for the first ever time, my grandma. He wanted her to see his new life and to show off his family. He was proud, and now was the right time. I was so excited, but apprehensive at the same time. So many thoughts were rushing through my mind. I envisaged her to be like my nanny, a big character who was warm but crazy also. My little mind was working overtime, and I just could not wait. It was to be one of the biggest anti-climaxes of my life.

My dad had collected her from Heathrow airport. We had been given strict instructions to be on our best behaviour. We all had the best manners anyway and were always dressed immaculately. It should have been wonderful. My grandma arrived.

She came into our house, and I really was not prepared for her at all. She was short and stout with thick glasses, but what struck me more was the coldness of her manner. The lack of her emotion permeated the entire room. She looked me up and down like I had messed on her shoe.

She stood by the fireplace whilst we were all sat on the settee. My dad kept it light and small talk was exchanged. It was uncomfortable and awkward, and you could have cut the air with a knife. My dad went and spoke with her on his own and came back with a pound note for us all from her. We all thanked her in unison, so politely and angelically. I could see my dad was proud of us, but I felt so sorry for him, for I had seen him take the pound notes out of his own pocket.

After everything, he wanted us to be left with a happy memory of her. It made me feel so sad for him and I knew even at the young age of seven why he didn't and couldn't maintain a relationship with his ma. My dad had to drop her back to Heathrow airport, and I went in the car with them. The atmosphere was frosty, but polite exchanges were made throughout the journey. My grandma offered me a sweet and I accepted by thanking her by her Christian name. My dad corrected me instantly and told me to call her grandma; I quickly rectified the situation and thanked her in the name of grandma. This in itself tickled me, and I was laughing precariously inside. I mean Grandma; I had never even met her in my life!

My dad was quipping jokes all the way and she remained steely and unperturbed through the whole of the journey. I can honestly say I had never met anyone quite like her before and I had been taught by nuns!

My dad dropped her at the arrivals at the airport. There were no hugs or words of love, but she did say to my dad that I was bright and clever and considering I came from my mam, she was very impressed! I mean the sheer audacity and disdain of it. I actually despised her for that comment and when she went to shake my hand I turned away, furious and adamant that she was no grandma of mine!!

So that was that and we were to be on our way home. I could see the relief sag from my dad's shoulders immediately. He said to me later that he could not wait to see the back of the ole twat and we would never have to be on ceremony for no one ever again. I was to later find out that this was his last-ditch attempt to give his mam a chance. She could not abide that we were bastards (not born in wedlock, which I was not to find out until after my mam died) and that my mam wasn't a good enough catholic girl for my dad.

It was the last time he ever saw his ma. She was dead to him and in effect had only ever given birth to him; she had never been maternal in the slightest. I felt so very sad for my dad, all he wanted was recognition from his ma and all he was to get was rejection once again!

It was a dog-eat-dog world and things resumed back to normal. I had a party for my birthday and was allowed to invite two friends. We had the usual sandwiches, sausage rolls, ice cream and jelly. It was great fun and one of my birthday presents was a beautiful Cindy doll. The next day when I wanted to play with it, I could not find it. Someone had stolen it, and, in my heart, I knew who it was. It was one of the girls I had invited around for tea.

My dad was not happy and made me go and get it back. She was four years older than me, but age was just a number in my house. I went down to her house and knocked on her door and demanded my doll back. She started laughing and mocking me, she basically admitted that she had it, but that it was hers now. I ran back home crying.

My dad was not having any of my tears and told me I had stick up for myself. I must admit that when the tears had subsided, I became overtaken by the sheer wrongness of it. I would have to have it out with her.

A couple of days later she came up my end of the street and my dad was out in the front garden with his arms folded watching what occurred. Do not get me wrong, I did not want to fight. It made me feel terrible inside, but where we came from it was the only way. This girls parents were people of no moral conscience, they gave their children nothing, hence why she had nicked my Cindy doll in the first place. She was a lot taller than me, obviously as she was four years older. It was now or never.

I gave her a good hiding. She stood no chance, and later that day I had my Cindy doll back. It may sound extreme to many people now, but that is how it was done back in our day.

My youngest brother and I were not allowed out of the street for the first six months or so and my sister had a fight arranged with a friend she had fallen out with. She arranged the fight over the road from the top of our street so we could watch. The fight ensued whilst my brother and I chanted our sister's name in unison, as loudly and as encouraging as we possibly could.

The other girl had brought everyone she knew, but my sister was on her own. She absolutely annihilated the other girl, but the girl did not take it well and told my sister she was going to get so and so (a lass who was a couple of years older than my sister and was the hardest girl in the district), so my sister said, "go and get her then".The girl was not happy, she had never lost a fight in her life and wanted my sister to pay.

Anyway, after a while this other girl arrived, possibly about a foot taller than my sister and twice as wide. The girl my sister had just fought with was looking with her face to my sister as if to say, 'right you are going to get it now"! The big girl was wearing orange socks and I remember as clear as day, my brother shouting, 'you orange sock bitch, leave my sister alone"!

We were of no use whatsoever. It's daft really, as we were too scared to leave the street but there was our sister across the road about to be slayed by this absolute giant and our parents had no clue!

We need not have worried though, as my sister tore her to pieces whilst the other girl's entourage looked on utterly gob smacked and in sheer disbelief. I must say, I completely shared their sentiment.

My brother and I were victorious, whilst my sister nonchalantly made her way back over the road to us. We were triumphant in her huge victory, and I felt so proud of her. Not only did she not have one friend beside her, but she held her nerve with so much dignity and composure, when I know deep down, she was scared! She thanked us for being there and said she could not have done it without us. Then off we all went back home without our mam and dad knowing absolutely nothing!

There were some funny memories as always from our time in the house. I remember my mam and dad would go out on the odd occasion and one of the times was near to Christmas. My eldest brother was always left in charge, and it was never long before carnage would ensue.

This one night my sister had decided to get her Christmas presents out of wherever they were hidden. It was a record player and she just sat there playing her records brazenly. My brother told her to put it back and she refused point blank. The next thing a full-scale fight erupted.

I was shouting for my brother to win, whilst my younger brother was favouring our sister, this generally was always the case though, (me backing my brother). My brother would always win and then like nothing had happened, everything was just how it was!

I did not tell my mam. I did not want to make her sad. She always went to great lengths to ensure we had a magical Christmas. The night before any Christmas day she would ask us all where we would want our presents leaving from Father Christmas and we would all pick a spot. Later we would hear him 'HO, HO, HO", and either my eldest brother or sister would proclaim that it sounded just like our dad!

The next day we would all wake far too early and gingerly creep down the stairs. We would then hear our mam shout, 'Get back to bloody bed, it's way too early" and we would all scramble straight back upstairs to bed, until a far more reasonable time. We would have everything we wanted, and I always knew and felt I was lucky!

One time near to Christmas my mam had sent my sister and I to the shop. My sister was not happy about this and whilst I was chirping on about Father Christmas, she stopped me dead in my tracks and as straight faced as you like told me there was no such thing as Father Christmas. I was beside myself. She warned me if I told me mam, she would kill me, but as soon as we got home, I ran crying to me mam!

She was so calm and cool, and as quickly as my words were out, she pacified me immediately! Of course, he was real, he had just fallen down a snowy slope that year and broken his leg. I was completely satisfied and placated by that explanation.

My sister was given a good crack for that one and even though I got the menacing look as if to say she was going to have me for it, she never did, thankfully.

The carol singers would come around and this one time my mam had asked my sister to answer the door. She did just that and chucked a bucket of water all over them whilst she was at it! She probably thought it was funny and to be honest, so did I, but it was not received that way.

My sister was unpredictable, and you never knew what was going on in her head. My mam used to call her dolly daydream as she liked to tell fabricated stories that would often filter their way back to my mam. One specific time at school she had embellished the furnishings of our house and had implied we had a phone in every room.

My mam had got wind of this and when asking my sister to fetch something from upstairs on one occasion, proceeded to call after her to be careful not to

trip over all the telephone wires on her way! My sister got it straightaway, and they just laughed!

My sister liked material things, always the nice clothes and jewellery, she was quite the Magpie! It was her form of escapism and her way of getting noticed also.

My mam was strutting around like a peacock in her new abode and in no time had my dad up the ladders painting and decorating. He was versatile my dad and could put his hand to pretty much anything.

I do not think my mam realised at this time though, the true extent of his gambling and soon the cracks started to appear. The late-night drunken antics began!

Our world was about to change once again.

I remember my mam hiding in the wardrobe one night. My dad was on his way back from the pub and the tension was formidably brewing. It was obvious if he could not find her, he would come looking for her and so he did! I remember the panic rising in my chest; they were going to kick off! None of us kids would say anything; we would just sit and listen to them shouting at the tops of their voices, whilst furniture was being thrown around. It is terrifying as a kid to hear and witness these things and no matter what, instinctively I would always feel protective over my mam.

My dad in his drunken state would then call us all down and ask us who we were going to live with. That was always the worst part though. I knew it would be my mam and I would not want to say so, as I did not want to hurt my dad. It was horrible and happened on more than one occasion. Once, they had a curry fight and the house stunk the next day. It was all up the landing walls, and it took my mam hours to clean it.

Looking back now, it was all spiralling out of control, and they were both desperately trying to cling onto the fairy-tale fragments that were left of the new house, new beginning charade!

The next day, after the arguments, they would try and paper over it and turn it into some sort of a joke. I might have been eight years old, but I knew joke and to me it just wasn't funny. I had a foreboding feeling circling around in my little tummy. I knew we were heading for a crash as a family, but did not quite know where, when or how!

My mam was still very close to her younger sister and would often be over her house or my nannies at weekends. Every so often they would come to ours. One night my nanny (who had by then, fostered my eldest auntie's two oldest children) and my aunty who had three children all came to stay. That night, my mam and dad kicked off again and we all fled the house in our pyjamas! Nobody had a car, and it was two different bus rides away back to my aunties. It was not until we were on the bus that nanny realised, she didn't have the two grandchildren with her!!

They had slept through the lot. We all laughed so hard at this. My family could find something funny in any event. A coping mechanism, I believe.

I remember my mam and nanny concocting the story, that when they fled the house and my dad slammed the door, it had whacked nanny's head on the back. I was not happy about it and shouted at my mam that she was lying, because they were.

My mam told me I did not understand, but I did. It was plainly obvious that the situation was bad enough, but they had to add more to justify their perspective of just how bad things were.

There was no denying that my dad's drinking was taking its toll on us all as a family. I was not a nervous person, nor were any of us, but the anticipation of what state he would be coming home in started to fill me with so much trepidation and anxiety. I did not want arguments; I wanted my parents to be happy.

I would often go up to my brother or sisters room and ask to get in their bed with them as I would be frightened. My sister would always tell me to 'fuck off," but my eldest brother would always let me in. He would just pull back the covers and that was it.

We never spoke to each other about it. None of us did but we all knew it was bad. My sister could barely cope with the situation herself, so she did not have the capacity to help me.

I felt ashamed and afraid that something terrible was going to happen. I know we all just wanted it to stop, and even at such a young age I was gauging my life against my friends. Their lives seemed to be perfect. I would never tell a soul though as I knew I could not.

One night we were all in bed, I would not sleep until I heard my dad come through the door. This was partly because I felt if he started on my mam, I would be able to protect her somehow. I was worrying constantly, but still in the process trying to maintain on the outside that all was good. Anyway, this night he arrived home and was covered in bandages.

His face was covered in bruises and was probably twice the size as it normally was. I was absolutely devastated to see him so vulnerable and pathetic. I ran to him to cuddle him. My first instinct was that he had been beaten up, but he had actually been in a collision in his car. A huge crash!

He was extremely lucky. He had collided head on with another vehicle whilst being intoxicated to oblivion! Seat belts were not compulsory back then, and drink driving was usually dealt with a slap on the wrist.

How he did not die, I will never know, but his guardian angel was watching over him that night for sure.

His actions were soaring out of control, and it was not long after that, we disintegrated as a family. The family crash came!

The house was being repossessed. My dad had not paid the mortgage. He was drinking heavily to mask the fact that he had plummeted into heavy debt.

His Achilles heel had eventually squandered his dreams.

He was no more than a gambling man who had in effect made his family homeless. The horses he had so frivolously invested in had not been kind to him; they had stabbed him so drastically in his heart, that he would have to inevitably pay for it for the rest of his life!

My mam was crestfallen and from then on, there was no going back. Her and my dad was breaking up. She could not endure any more heart ache. Even though she loved him still, it was not enough anymore, and she was adamant to do right for us kids.

I though, could not have cared less about what was right!

The tears cascade,

Avalanching into an infinite why well.

It is a bottomless pit of whys.

Holding not a morsel of solace for the countless lies.

The why well plunges severely deep.

There is no consolation left to reap.

FIVE

GOODBYES

Mam broke the news that my dad and her were breaking up! My little heart shattered. I was a daddy's girl through and through. My dad had never raised his voice to me. When my mam would send him to discipline me, he would put his hand on me, smack it, then gesture for me to pretend to cry! As a child, you desperately want your parents to stay together. I loved them both. Something inside me knew my dad would not cope well. It was devastating!

That was only the first part of the blow. We were going to be moving into my aunt's house. So not only were my parents breaking up, but we also had to leave our house and move in with my aunty and her three kids. Not only that, my nanny and her two fostered kids (her grandchildren, my cousins) lived there too. Now, five more and a dog were adding to it!

It was a tiny three-bedroom council house. You could barely swing a cat in there, let alone have it-inhabit twelve people! It was a tiny three bedroomed council house.

My life was about to embark on a whole new chapter that was to give me some of the best memories, but also some of the saddest!!

The day we left my dad was like my soul had been destroyed to say the least. When you are wrenched away from someone you love, it leaves an everlasting impact. I was angry, but I knew I had to keep it bottled inside as emotional displays were not acceptable within our family.

My mam ever the trouper, gave me a cuddle and held me for a few minutes in a reassuring it's 'going to be ok hold. She knew how I was feeling, and that supportive little display of love meant everything to me. My mam never exposed any chinks in her armour. Stiff upper lip and all that! I can honestly say I never seen my mam crumble under any circumstance, and she was not going to start now.

Our belongings were put into storage and in we all moved to my aunts. I was placed in a school almost immediately, only until a suitable catholic school could take me in. That happened a week later! I hated it there.

The 'cock" of the school, the bully, decided to make me his target. I will never forget him. He had a big mouth and basically ruled the school with fear and terror. Everyone was frightened of him. He was an abhorrent young lad and had not an ounce of integrity in his whole. I loathed him, everyone did, and it did not matter how invisible I tried to make myself, it just made me seem even more noticeable to him. I was going home every day consumed by him, but it was not because I was scared of him. It was because I was scared of what I was going to do to him!

I could not talk to anyone. For one, that is not what I did (I always kept my troubles to myself) and also, I really didn't want to trouble my mam with everything she had going on, so I just kept all the turmoil rolling around inside.

By then I had developed little boobs, and this was to be the straw that broke the camel's back. The bully decided to make a grab for them one day. I had had enough! I beat the living daylights out of him.

He got all my bottled-up feelings exploding all over his face and, as predicted, I was perfectly within my right to be worried about what I would do to him! He was quite a mess after it.

To see this huge cock turn into the little coward, he actually was, was really quite sad! I just remember as clear as day, him holding onto his nose and there was blood all over his shirt. His eyes were all red and puffy, and his hair was a complete mess.

Funnily enough, he left me and everyone else alone after that. I had shamed him in the worst possible way and probably taught him one of the biggest lessons of his life. I remember feeling really sorry for him, sorry that it had come to that, but he did not heed the warnings I was giving him, and I had given him plenty. I was not proud of it at all because it really was shameful, but you cannot be who you are not, and I just wasn't born to take shit from nobody. All I wanted was to be left alone and just to be happy.

After the deed was done, I felt free again and it enabled me to concentrate on what I really loved, which was my education. I started to over exceed in my academic ability! I loved learning, and something inside me was not going to let anyone spoil my desires and happiness. My life's experiences had instilled so much inside of me already and my parents had taught me the only way to deal with a bully was to take them on. I was a nice girl, but my parents had taught me that you have to stand up for yourself and that is the way they taught me do it!

There was an awful lot occurring for a young mind to comprehend. The vast changes had changed me. I was way older than my years and for a young girl of eight years old, my wisdom and resoluteness unnerved many people around me.

My mam and dad remained on good terms for us. By then, my dad had a found a flat and would come and collect me and my youngest brother most weekends to stay with him. That was my salvation and something I could look forward to. I could not help but feel sorry for him still. He had a good heart, and anybody could see that he still loved my mam.

He always remained fun, and my brother and I were in our element whilst with him. He would spoil us and most importantly wanted to know everything about us. Emotionally, I always felt valid when I was in his company. He would ensure that we never had to worry and his love for us was illuminating and authentic to the core. He was my light and I loved him. Regardless of his weaknesses he only ever showed strength and love to me.

His flat was by a little beck which had speckle back fish in it. On this one occasion when my brother and I were going to stay, I had bought myself a little fishing net so to catch them. I was so smug about it as it was all shiny and new, and my brother did not have one.

My nanny though, was not having it. She decided to make my brother his own out of an old broomstick, a coat hanger and some butcher's mesh. It looked awful. Nothing like my brand-new, perfect, shop bought net. I was smirking at my brother and relishing (over zealously) in having the best.

We went off with my dad, hurriedly down to the beck we scarpered to catch the speckle back and tadpoles. To my utmost horror, when we got there, my brother was catching all of them, my net was useless as the holes were too big! I was humiliated and angry.

My brother savoured every single second of it, as you can imagine! It taught me a very valuable lesson that day. New and shiny can be futile, all that glitters is not gold. For some reason, I was quite a snob. I learned quite a few lessons this way throughout my life. I could be very condescending and patronising towards my little brother, but every once in a while, I would receive a lesson like this one and he absolutely gloated over it! It was not often anyone could get one over on me!

Another time at my dad's, we made a milkshake and decided to chuck it out of the window (which was about the tenth floor up) to see if we could get it on the horse down below. We succeeded in our target, but of course, mayhem erupted! We denied it was us, but my dad knew and acted like he did not.

He was soft with us and to be honest, he encouraged that behaviour in us. He would never make us feel bad about anything; to him we were just kids being kids and I loved him for that.

My mam on the other hand, would have killed us!!

It was hectic at my aunties. There was no space to think. I felt I was judged from the minute I got there. I was deemed spoilt, sly, and too clever for my own good. I heard things about me whilst listening behind closed doors and caught little snippets whilst sitting on the bottom of the stairs ear wigging.

It was, in a way, soul destroying! I just wanted my mam and dad back together. I did not want to be there. I had gone from having my own room to

five of us sharing a bed! I was not spoilt or snobby; I was just missing my old life and my dad!

There was competitiveness between my mam and her sister, and it was usually to do with me. Whilst the other kids would be out playing, I would be sat at the table with my mam. I was close to her and liked to be near her, but this was deemed as me being nosey and spoilt.

I could not help but be protective over my mam. I wanted to make sure she was ok. Looking back now, I can see I had developed anxiety, and she was my comfort blanket. Everything about my feelings was dismissed.

Not once did my aunty ever give me a cuddle, apart from the one time I was due to get a good hiding from my mam and it was my aunty that had instigated that hiding. I felt she hated me for some reason.

I realised after a conversation later in life, she actually felt she did! I was taking too much of mam's time when she believed she was much more important. Now that I am a mother myself, it breaks my heart to know just how selfish she was. I was getting in the way of my mams attentions towards her!

My children are everything to me. They become above and beyond anything and anyone (even my husband). We both know it, as he feels the same way too!

As children, you quickly soon adapt and develop a surprising bounce back ability. Before long you adjust, and everything feels like it has always been that way. Playing out on the streets with my cousins and meeting new kids was fantastic.

My aunty lived next door to a family, who had a daughter, who would later become a huge star (in one of the biggest girl bands). I became really friendly with her. She was quite a lot like me, very confident, mischievous, scary* but funny. She was more of a dancer though, as I was the singer. My younger brother would kiss her in the alley whilst I kept watch.

It was quite a new estate and fairly big, so there was always someone to play with. Every now and then, someone would get hold of two skipping ropes. We would spend hours doing double Dutch whilst someone blared out Malcom Mclaren from a ghetto blaster. Music was always playing somewhere in the background and generally, it was reggae.

Bob Marley, Buffalo Soldier would come on and all of us kids would just sing along to it, at the top of our voices, in the middle of the street, just loving every minute of it!

Every now and then I would round all the kids up with my guitar and play songs (daddies taking us to the zoo, she sat neath the lilacs, just to name a few) and get them all to sing along. This was much to their great dissatisfaction and dismay, but they would not argue with me and if they got a note wrong, I would scold them awfully! All of us together were a formidable force and there were no questions asked. We ruled!

I loved all my cousins and always will do.

All of my cousins possessed a special substance about them. My oldest cousin was the one I looked up to the most. She was beautiful with dark ringlets in her hair. She was studious and liked to learn; she was wise beyond her years. She was five years older than me, and I would observe her admirably from afar. I liked her style, and her overall persona was poised and calm. She was always lovely to me too. She became an avid influence on me, and she is someone to this day whom I admire.

Another one of my cousins was like no other I had ever met, or ever have. He was a year younger than me, and he was the funniest, cheekiest, most charismatic little soul you could ever meet. He was always up to no good. Stealing, running away from the coppers (who could never catch him).

He would play my nanny up to high heaven. She would lock him out of her house, and he would shout through the letterbox to be let back in. Nanny would shout "Fuck off home you little black bastard!" Nobody else would have ever dared do that, eventually she would let him back in, they would have a cuddle, and all would be forgiven.

He was my other auntie's son, so he did not live with us, but everyone knew when he was around. He had a heart of gold and would give you anything if he could. His vibe was infectious, and he would have you laughing constantly. He was so good looking, and all the girls gravitated towards him. He was bright and extremely clever and never nasty (well, not to the ones he loved). My mam absolutely adored him, and the feeling was mutual between them. She knew things about him and his life, and she had a very special place in her heart for him. He was her little darling.

My mam loved every single one of her nieces and nephews very deeply.

Easter was approaching and we were all looking forward to our chocolate eggs. Money was tight and luxuries were off limits, so the prospect of having some chocolate in our bellies was thrilling.

We all awoke Easter morning and went to get our eggs out of the fridge. The boxes were there, but the foils were empty! Pandemonium erupted!

Nanny was shouting at the top of her voice "Which greedy bastard ate the fucking Easter Eggs?" It was rather obvious that the culprits weren't going to confess, but we all had a very strong inkling to who they were. We kids were all devastated, but mostly, we were absolutely fuming!

By the end of the day, the Easter egg thieves had been sought out and were punished with a good hiding!

We all knew exactly who they were though, it was always the same two, my youngest brother and one of my other cousins. The pair of them were always up to something, which usually involved something to do with nicking!

It makes me laugh out loud when I think of this memory!

Everyone was scared stiff of my nanny! She took no shit off no one, and everybody knew it on our estate. She liked to sit around her round table smoking and drinking tea (in the daytime) and special brew at night. She liked us grandchildren to run around after her and specially to make her cups of tea.

She would never ask though, instead she would initiate the drumming of her fingers on the round table. When that did not fetch the right response, she would then start tapping her fingers loudly, then the loud sighs would commence, and if she had not had a reaction by then, her foul mouth would then kick in and all Mary hell would break loose!

We were all selfish little bastards and she had had enough of the fucking lot of us, she was an old lady (55ish I would guess), and nobody gave a fuck about her, we were little cunts, and we could all fuck off!!

The thing is, we all knew the signs and generally more often than not, one of us would intercept before she lost it, by making her a cup tea by the time the tapping was underway. Every now and then though, we would want her to kick off. She was never frightening with it or scary. As bad as it sounds, she was absolutely hilarious, and we would all be hid in the front room rolling around in hysterics.

Eventually, one of us would calm her down and make a fuss out of her. Whoever it was, she would tell them that they were her favourite grandchild and always had been!

The funniest times were when she was obliterated under the influence of alcohol. This one time, she went to meet her friend down the pub and came back absolutely steaming. Unbeknown to us, she thought she had put a chicken in the oven to roast before she had gone out. Any-way, she comes in and opens the cooker to discover that the chicken is missing! She went completely mental, screaming at top decibel 'Who's nicked the fucking chicken!"

None of us had a clue what she was on about and were looking at one another like she had lost the plot. I mean, she was shrieking so loud the whole estate must have heard her. We kids though, were just falling about, in absolute stitches, laughing our heads off. Finally, after a lot of banging and crashing around, she found the chicken in the cupboard. She had put it into the cupboard instead of in the oven before she went out (she was half cut then!).

She would never admit she was in the wrong though and was insistent that it was one of us little bastards. If it were one of my cousins, then they would be screamed at as little 'black bastards." I mean we all laugh about it even until this day, but what nanny shouts that?

Our nanny did. She was really something else.

It was not long before my nanny had her own council house given to her, which just happened to be six doors down from aunty. It was so exciting. She had all new everything put in and it was absolutely stunning. More so my cousins, whom she fostered would now get their own rooms, which at the time it obviously meant more room for all of us. Things were looking up and decisions were being made to shape all of our futures.

My nanny was soft though, and even though she was neurotic and crazy, she had a way of making me feel special. I loved her with all my heart and I knew she loved me. Even more so the day my mam broke the news that we were moving away!

My first thought was of my dad. How far away was Devon? Could I still see him at weekends? What about my family, my nanny and my cousins? Again, I was preparing myself for the unknown. My mam had her mind set. She wanted a new start.

When my mam and my dad were younger, they had stayed in a caravan in Devon - whilst my dad was doing some roadworks. Whilst there, my mam had met a lifelong, lovely friend. They never lost contact and had obviously been talking with each other. Her friend had a guest house and invited my mam and us to stay.

I will never forget the day I had to say goodbye to my dad. He came to my nanny's new council house. I wanted to tell him I loved him and just did not know how. My nanny had picked up on this and asked me what was wrong. I whispered that I wanted to tell my dad that I loved him. She grabbed my hands and hugged me tight and whispered back "You go tell him, tell him how much you love him and hug him with your all your heart! Go on, you do it!"

With those words whispered, that is exactly what I did. My dad picked me up and swung me around, and instantaneously his posture changed from a heartbroken man to a man with hope!

He hugged me hard, and I cried tears of happiness (for telling him) and such sadness (that I would be leaving him).

This was to be the last time I was to see my dad before we left.

I will never forget that hug until the day I die and the look of love of my nanny 's face!

Cling to this moment and hold onto it tight.

This memory forever will remain in my sight.

It will be sacredly guarded.

Implanted in my soul.

Protected so fiercely.

Etched into my whole.

Embedded into my heart.

From now until eternity.

My love for you all will last to infinity.

SIX

DEVON

I have to say at this time in my life I felt like I hated my mam. Why was she uprooting us so drastically? Tearing us away from all we knew and loved. I mean Devon, 260 miles away. I did not understand distances back then, but my gut was telling me it was far, far away. She may as well have moved us to Timbuktu for all I cared, and I remember vividly thinking that (why Timbuktu I do not know).

We could have filled a small pond with the number of tears that were shed between us all when saying our goodbyes. My Nannies face on that day is still etched so distinctly into my mind's eye. It really was of sheer heart break and sorrow, and it resonated so profoundly within me. I really believe she felt my mam would change her mind at the last minute and I think we all echoed that sentiment, but it was not to be. My aunty just cried relentlessly, sobbing unashamedly and again we all followed suit.

Inside I felt desolate and inconsolable and even more so as my oldest brother had decided to stay with my dad. He was 13 and did not want to leave his friends behind! He meant the world to me; he was just so kind and thoughtful towards me. I adored him and I felt like another chunk of my heart was being wrenched away. Again, though it had to be contained, and I had to compartmentalise it, in another little box in my brain.

This must have been incredibly hard for my mam, and it was not until years later that I realised that my mam did not do a thing just for herself. Everything she did was to give us a better life. It must have taken a lot of determination and strength to do what she did. She had a plan and that was that! Her mind was made up and by hook or crook she was intent on succeeding.

The train journey was a mix of emotions. My mam was bright and optimistic about our new life ahead. I knew inside I had to come to terms with the whole thing because when my mam made her mind up, there was no going back!

As a child I had an amazing ability to look for the good in things and adapt to situations almost instantly. There was no choice, so you had to get on with it. Like it or lump it!

As we approached Devon, I started to feel a tingle of hope as the train trundled along by the sea. It was the beginning of the summer and my mam had filled us with all the positives of living by the coastline!

We must have looked like complete delinquents on that train, my younger brother and I began jumping up and down on our seats, squealing with delight at the sight of the sea.

Although we had holidayed in Devon in years gone by, we had never travelled on the train and seen the sheer magnitude of the beauty of the sea- that it held whilst passing it by. My sister was not amused by this, we were an embarrassment, I am sure. She was way to cool for those displays.

Even the dog was excited, he always knew what was going on did that dog. He was way more knowing than a dog should have been and would always participate in the relevant emotion at any given time.

My mam took upmost joy in this outburst and whilst others on that journey were wanting their peace, my mam sat back and enjoyed every minute of her children being happy. It was something she had not seen in quite a while, and she was holding onto every second.

Till this day I still feel that same emotion when I travel on the train to the nearby destinations that I am lucky to be surrounded with. I did not know it at the time, but that summer was to be one of the best of my life!

My mams friend was a lovely, warm lady. She had four children, two boys and two girls but I was particularly fond of her youngest daughter. She had stayed with us in Leeds when she was pregnant with her first child, and she would send me down to the greengrocers for bananas. She must have had a craving for them as that is all she seemed to eat. She was funny and kind and had a big heart. She took me and my youngest brother under her wing almost immediately and made everything fun for us.

We were a handful, to put it mildly, and together we were like the terrible twins. Because there was not much of an age gap between us, we were often mistaken for twins from as far back as I can remember. We had the cutest little faces and looked like little angels. Together though, we were little devils. We had seen a lot and were very streetwise. We would run rings round anyone, if we thought we could get away with it and unfortunately for my mam's friends daughter, she fit all the criteria down to a T.

Where we were staying was not very far from the beach, but it was a bit of a walk amongst some busy roads. As it was summer, pretty much every day was spent there. It was like a long holiday and my mam made sure it felt like that. We were having a whale of time and whilst I had my little brother, I also had a best friend. We did everything together. Most of the time we would get on fine, but on occasions we would fight and could be nasty with it! We were extremely stubborn, there was no doubt we loved each other but when the fight for survival kicked in, the love evaporated into thin air.

My brother definitely had more of the killer instinct in him, I was just lucky that I was tougher than him then. In later years he gained respect for me. Which I am very thankful about.

My mum 's friend 's daughter would take us to the beach most of the time. She had a young baby and it suited her to get out of the house. My brother and I would spend all day in the sea, only coming out when we were hungry. We were as good as gold when it suited us but when she decided it was time to go home, we had decided we just were not ready to leave!

We would not come out of the sea and no matter what she threatened us with or tried to entice us with, it just would not work. Eventually we would give up, but only when we were ready. She would be absolutely fuming and completely exasperated, as you can imagine.

I think the first time we were being naughty and trying our luck, she went to give us a whack; well, we caused such a commotion, screaming at the top of our voices that she was battering us and trying to kidnap and kill us and that we just wanted our mam, and that she wasn t our mam. Everyone around was staring at her, and us. It became evident to all surrounding us that we were feral, little scoundrels and nobody bothered to intervene. The thing is she was a well-known girl, and the locals knew what the score was!

She never tried to whack us again, but we paid for it later from our mam and we had an almighty whack from her instead. She was livid! How dare could we have behaved so appallingly when the girl had taken us to beach when she did not have to! It certainly made us think twice in the future though. My mam was not to be showed up!

Still, the lovely girl that she was, she was always quick to forgive us. I think she also found us funny, and cheeky above all. I saw her like a big sister and still feel love for her to this day!

The other sister was a different ball game altogether. She was cold and unsurprisingly so. She was a lot older and had no time for little people. She was not a nasty person by far, but we were of no significance in her life and annoyed her. She kept a big jar of bon bons in her bedroom and every so often would offer me one. I loved bon bons and relished in her kindness.

One time though, I thought I would help myself; I crept into her room and only took one, but she caught me red handed. She slapped me hard around the face and it hurt. She shouted to me that I was a greedy little bitch, and I would never have one of her bon bons again. Well after that I did not want one of her bon bons and I kept a very wide berth from her in the future. I did not like her from that day onwards and never forgot either.

Yes, I was in the wrong, but to slap me around the face was a bit overzealous and harsh. I could not tell my mam though, as she would have whacked me for nicking in the first place. I just had to take it on the chin.

I know though if a person had ever laid their hands on me for no reason, my mam would have absolutely wiped the floor with them, and I so wanted my mam to wipe the floor with her!

The thing is though as I got older, I learnt that about myself, if you wronged me, I would never forget and found it harder to forgive. I could not make excuses for wrongful behaviour in any way and if anyone went against my moral code, I could cut them off without a backward glance.

My brother and I were proper little terrors though, and together we were always up to something or another. I do not know what possessed us, but one day we decided we would open all the residents mail. It was not just my mams friend and family that lived there, other people lodged there also. We did this for about two weeks concurrently and would rip it all in to tiny shreds and then bin it. It was only when one of the residents who was expecting a cheque in the post became suspicious that something fishy was going on. He caught us in the act the following morning and we had ripped his cheque to pieces.

He was livid and so was my mam! We each had an almighty whack around the head and were not allowed out for a couple of days. The thing is, we did not read the mail and did not deem that actually what we were doing was wrong, it just felt like fun at the time!

Another time we were all down the beach and my brother and I had been sent to fetch fish and chips. It was quite a walk, and the fish shop was closed. For some unfathomable reason I decided it would be funny that on arriving back I would hide behind the wall that led onto the beach, whilst my brother ran onto the beach to my mam shouting that I had been knocked down. The logic behind it was that I would then jump out and shout 'Surprise" and everyone would start laughing and we would be hailed as cheeky little buggers!

Oh no, that was not to be so. My mam had gone into sheer panic mode and so had everyone else on the beach, she was up on her feet running to find me and when I popped out shouting 'surprise" the look on her face was not of pleasure or amusement, it was of pure anger and embarrassment.

I had seen that look many times before, but not as animated as this time. I knew instantly we were in for it big time. My brother got a whack straight away and she muttered to me through gritted teeth that I would be in for it later. I felt sick with anticipation and felt like my life would be over. I think that may have been the angriest I had ever seen her, especially because I had drawn attention to us, and all eyes were on her!

By the time we had made our way back home, my mams anger had subsided, and she just did not have the energy to blow it up again. I was damn lucky as I probably escaped the biggest hiding of my life.

Something inside me had learnt a very valuable lesson that day. I realised later when I became a parent the sheer terror she must have been feeling and what absolute little shits we actually were!!

There was an outdoor pool just up from the beach and we would just spend every minute in that pool. I was to suffer from the worst sunburn on my shoulders and I remember it peeling and all scabbing over, but I just wore a T-shirt over the top. Nothing was a big deal and we all just got on with things back then.

Yes, I know my mam felt bad about it and probably many other things too, but you just got on with it. We never sat down as a family and talked about feelings and whether that be right or wrong, it worked for most of the time with us. We were loved and even during the extreme turbulence of everything that had ever gone in my life, I always knew that.

The relationship with my sister was spasmodic to say the least. She did not like me and I, in turn, did not like her for not liking me. In a lot of ways, I was a proper goody two shoes, and it riled her. I was a tell-tale tit on her and because she was horrible to me, I would get my own back by telling on her at every golden opportunity. Whatever she did that was bad, I just could not wait to spill the beans.

This particular time, I had caught her smoking in the garden, and she bribed me by being nice not to tell my mam, but the minute she set a foot a wrong I ran to my mam and told her. It was pretty much how we were most of the time, and the only time she was ever nice to me was when I had something over her.

I did not realise at the time that my sister's issue was not actually really with me at all, but with how we were both treated so obviously differently. My dad made it very plain for all to see that I was the favourite, and she was not. From a child's perspective, I can understand the thought process. It must have been difficult for such a young mind to comprehend this, and her little

mind just could not. It was a terrible thing for my dad to do and the repercussions were already forming between mine and my sister's relationship. My self-esteem was brimming over, whilst my sister was struggling to keep herself sane at times.

Looking back now, it was nothing short of cruel, but I still believe that my dad in some way, or another was trying to toughen my sister up and my god he certainly accomplished that.

She became my parent's scapegoat, the one who would shoulder their shortcomings and misgivings in life. It was not until our later years we began to understand the profound effect it contributed to her mental health and the detriment it caused in her life choices!

I had two months of having a ball. It was hot, the sky was blue, the sun shone every day, and we were living by the sea. What more could a child want. It felt like a permanent holiday, and I was just enjoying being young and carefree and as we were so busy having fun,

I did not really have the time to miss my dad and my Leeds life. I think somewhere in my mind I believed we were going back and that was my little way of dealing with it. It worked.

Reality must kick in though eventually, and sooner rather than later, it did! We were moving again! My mam had found a winter let in a little village nearby.

Summer was coming to an end, and we were heading into September now and my tenth birthday was fast approaching. So many drastic changes had happened in my young years already, this again, was just another one of many!

The sunshine was mine today, only mine.

It rose big and yellow and was warm to me.

It invited me to a new world I had never known before; it was kind.

And I felt serene, and my mind was calm.

The sunshine enveloped my sorrows and made me smile.

The sunshine made me happy,

If only for a short while.

SEVEN

THE VILLAGE IDIOTS

The winter let was situated in a tiny village which could have been on the moon as far as I was concerned. It really was like nothing I had ever known. I at least was familiar with the seaside as we had holidayed in Devon as kids. This place was completely depressing to me.

The house was small, which was not anything new to me, but it was old and because autumn had arrived, it was particularly dark and sombre. It had a cold feeling about it. It was not welcoming in any way and in general I hated it. There were no streetlights, and we were surrounded by fields. I had never heard a cow moo or a sheep baa in real life before and they were noisy and scary at the same time.

I despised it and wanted desperately to return to the streets of Leeds. I was terribly homesick. My mam again remained upbeat and positive as she had to; she had brought us here after all and she had to show us it was all going to be fine, even though I believe she was having doubts herself!

It was, however, very difficult for me. I wanted my dad so badly that my heart was physically aching. I had a picture of him under my pillow and was crying myself to sleep every night. I know my mam knew this, but she could not show any weakness as we would have grounded her down. She had to remain strong and focused on the bigger picture. She knew what she was doing.

By then though she had started dating, and that is when the penny dropped that again there was no going back. We would speak to my dad and my brother once a week, so I just concentrated on that!

I was missing my brother badly also. It really was awful. I was sleeping in with my mam most nights by then. I think it was a comfort for her as much as for me, for even though she never let on until later years, she was terrified of the dark!

My mam decided after a night out one time to bring a man she had met, and obviously liked, back for a nightcap. I could never sleep until she was back and then suddenly, I heard this man's voice. I was absolutely furious! I could feel the rage burning inside me and I wanted him out. I leapt out of bed as fast as my little legs would carry me. Next minute, I am down the stairs and as my mam went to introduce him to me, I unleashed the rage!

46

To say my mam was mortified was an understatement. I screamed for him to get out of the house, that he was not my dad and that he was fucking old and ugly! I knew exactly what I was doing, and I wanted to make sure I did a good job of it! I called my mam every name under the sun and did not care less if she beat me or not. He was not my dad, and he was not welcome in the house.

I honestly do not think in all my life up until then, I had seen my mam speechless. She couldn t herself, quite believe what she had witnessed. She stood there with her mouth wide open, whilst he feebly mumbled excuses and made a dash for it!

He must have thought I was mental and that is precisely what I wanted him to think! I felt like I had achieved my goal and felt utterly smug about it, not for one minute longer though. I had an almighty whack around the head for that performance and was kicked up the stairs, straight into bed. By then, I realised the sheer magnitude of what I had done and I was terrified of the repercussions. I knew I had completely overstepped the mark, but still I was fervently proud of my outlandish, magnificent outburst and could only assume that my dear dad would have been ultimately proud of my Oscar winning act! It would have been worth the beating of my life, if only to wake my mam up out of whatever delusional mindset she seemed to be suffering from.

The next day my mam sat me down. She must have been up all-night thinking about it. She gave me a cuddle and a good talking to. She explained that she was going to meet someone else eventually and I had to accept it. She told me he would never replace my dad in any way, and she understood how I felt, but in a nice way of saying it, basically it was tough shit, and she wouldn t be standing for any more of my outbursts or nonsense.

I had turned ten by now and had started the village school. That was it. I made friends and the world seemed much brighter. My new best friend 's parents owned the local stables, so I had the luxury and pleasure of riding a horse for the first time. I was not feeling like an outsider anymore. I was always good at making friends and no matter what was going in my life, my confidence never wavered.

I think because I was so bright, school never phased me, so in a lot of ways I never had to worry about those things. I have always known also that most people like to laugh. Even if they do not know it, most people do. It is a universal connection that you can take anywhere and usually, all I would have to do is get that look from someone and the floodgates would open. It really is the best medicine and tonic for all.

There were, as always, funny times! My brother and I would take a neighbour's donkey out. It was very kind of them, and we loved it, we couldn't believe our luck, but as always it would turn into an argument of some sort. One day it was my turn on the donkey, and I had been on it way too long for my brother's liking (it was his turn).

He was getting fed up and bored and wanted his ride. We were right outside the village post office. He started acting up, insisting I got off. I would not, so he decided to lash out in temper.

With that, the donkey started bucking, winding him in his gut in the process. He was rolling around on the ground screaming whilst I was hanging onto that donkey for dear life. The commotion, in all its glory, had attracted quite a gathering and in the midst of the facade, someone had run up to our house to get my mam. She came running down absolutely fuming with that look that showed a thousand whacks were coming our way! I swear I saw steam coming out of her ears. We were in for it!!

We were marched home and once inside, both of us were whacked around the head. How dare we bring shame to her like that. We must have been the laughingstock of the whole village, and I am quite certain we were!

My brother had his pay back shortly after, much to my indignation. The owner of the donkey had a beautiful horse, and the donkey would follow that horse anywhere. When it was just the two of us and the donkey, it would blatantly stop dead in its tracks if he did not want to go any further. No amount of coercing or cajoling would get it to move. When he was following that horse though, he would turn into the equivalent of black beauty.

This one particular day, I was following them on my brother's BMX, and it was my turn. My brother was not playing turns, so off he and the donkey flew after the horse, up the highest of hills. There was no way the bike and my little legs would endure it. I succumbed with a heavy heart and a vengeance towards my brother and made my way home. My brother returned what felt like hours later with the smuggest look on his face. My mam was delighted for him, but I on the other hand was plotting my revenge!

We had a little stream running adjacent to the back of our garden and my brother and I would spend hours playing in there, pretending we were sailors or pirates. Our imaginations were resplendently unseen, and I hardly remember a time when we were bored.

There was a swing in our back garden too, but this caused many fights between us because quite frankly, we were not very good at sharing, and taking turns was something neither of us liked doing.

One particular day, my brother came running into the house beckoning for me to go on it. He was being so lovely, and it was to be one of the only times

I let my guard down. Inside something was telling me it was too good to be true, but I caved in.

Out I ran and plonked myself happily onto the swing, wrapped my hands around the sides but straight away my senses screamed to me something was not right. He had found two slow worms and wrapped them around either side. I hated them and he knew it and I screamed at the top of my lungs!

He took great satisfaction in his demon act and gloated laboriously for many years to come. It taught me to nurture my guard more finely. I was certain from that day on to be cautious about any niceties he would show me in future.

My brother had found a field whilst out exploring one day. It had two horses in this field, and he decided in his nine years of wisdom to ride one of these horses bareback. He came back a changed boy from that experience.

It turns out that the horses names were Bubbles and Crackers and the one he nearly broke his neck on was of course, Crackers! It was named Crackers because it was Crackers, and he was exceptionally lucky to make it out alive! No one would even ride that horse with a saddle on!

My mam decided it would be good for my brother and I to get involved in the village way of life and the pair of us were invited to participate in the bell ringing at the local church. We were not entirely enthralled by the prospect, but we wouldn t have argued with our mam.

We arrived at the church and were greeted warmly and wholeheartedly by the other bell ringers. They were older than us and were very serious indeed about the structure and formation of the procedure it entailed. They took their time to show us the ropes so to speak. How we pulled them down and how to let them go. Then pull them back down and take hold of them at a certain part of the rope. It was a rather enjoyable experience and I mastered it on the first try. My brother soon got into the swing of it also.

We though, got bored quite quickly and decided it would be way more fun to try our own way. Basically, we pulled the rope down and seen if we could go back up with it. That technique failed, unfortunately. We then pulled the rope back down and let go of it completely. We knew exactly what we were doing but acted so innocently in the process.

I believe they knew what we were doing also, as we were never invited back again. We just had to push everything to the extreme.

Money was tight for my mam, and she had decided to take the bull by the horns and approach the village shop for tick (buy now, pay later scheme). She was a proud woman, but when the need was a must, she would get on and sort it. They had no idea what tick meant down the shop but after my mam explained about our situation and how and when she would pay, they accepted.

My mam was not looking for pity and her integral communication would have represented this so, to her she was simply negotiating a scenario that would work for her. She would always pay.

Afterwards, we all laughed. It takes some audacity to do what she did and even though I cringed at the prospect, I also understood that was what she did and had to do, in order to survive and make sure we never went without.

As money was tight, my brother and I came up with a stupendous plan of picking the lock on the electricity meter. Not to steal the money, we weren t thieves; but we thought that by repeatedly putting a fifty pence through the meter, at a very rapid rate was an exceptional plan, but we had to be snappy before my mam came back from the shop.

I swear we must have put that same fifty pence piece through, at least a hundred times. We were beyond jubilant with our performance; our mam would not have to put electric money in for months and we were ultimately proud of ourselves for saving her some money!

She on the other hand did not share our triumph, she went bat - shit crazy! She put on every electrical appliance as to spin the meter as fast as possible to reduce the amount. We (in our stupidity) did not think about the bigger picture, that the landlord visited weekly to empty the meter and he knew pretty much how much would be in there. My mam was petrified we were going to be evicted. I swear we got a proper good hiding for that shenanigan. Thankfully, her quick thinking seemed to deal with the situation and fortunately for us, the landlord was completely oblivious. He was in fact a gentleman my mam said, and probably more the reason she did the right the thing!

We really were proper naughty but most of the time it was with the best intentions! One day we were all sat around joking and contemplating about who we thought was the village idiot (there was a few suitable candidates) whilst laughing our heads off. Suddenly, my mam went quiet and looked at us all and said, 'Do you know what, we are sat here laughing at them, but I bet everyone else has us down as the village idiots." We all burst out laughing again. We most definitely must of been deemed the prize winning 'Village Idiot's '. She had a very valid point!

We were like aliens there and we could have quite easily been living on the moon!

There were times when my brother and sister would go off together (purposely to exclude me) and one of the times, I found them with a Thomas cookbook. My sister had sworn my brother to secrecy, but he later on he confided in me that they were planning on running away (back to Leeds) and my sister had it all worked out.

I never told on her for that, as I understood. I was just more hurt that I was not allowed to join. It never happened though, but how sad.

It made me think of my brother up in Leeds. He would not have left me out and I missed him so much. It was times like that, the enormity of the sadness would engulf me. We were all broken in our own ways. The pain plunged deeply.

The dog would still walk himself. He liked to familiarise himself with new surroundings, like you do. We were all completely blasé about village life, ignorant really.

Unbeknown to us, the dog had been chasing after the sheep in the nearby fields and had been shot at twice! We only knew about this because the farmer had tracked us down and turned up on our doorstep. He was downright angry!

My mam though, she had him eating out of the palm of her hand within minutes. She had him worked out within seconds and had reeled him in with her excessive charm. By the time he was leaving they were laughing and joking, and he even patted the dog on the head when he left.

As bad as it sounds, we still never walked the dog after that incident, but he knew the mayhem he had caused and stopped chasing the sheep. He always knew!

My mam went out one evening and again my brother and I got into a fight. In the process of this fight, we smashed one of our mams beloved blue and white China ornaments. The head came clean off and we automatically went from fighting into sheer panic and terror as to how we were going to rectify this major disaster. We could not find any super glue, so it was decided that I would have to go knocking on the neighbour's doors in the pitch black to find someone who had.

Miraculously, the first door I knocked on, a lady answered and happened to have some. I ran home elated and exuberant in the fact we could now mend our mams precious ornament. I glued it as precisely as possible, and we both relished in our achievement.

My brother and I could fight like hyenas one minute and be the best of allies in the next, especially when it came down to serious business. We were a puzzling, peculiar pair of siblings.

Anyway all was wonderful, until the neighbour pulled my mam aside a couple of days later and asked her if the super glue was of any use. My mam put two and two together and knew exactly what had happened! She was angrier that I had supposedly been out roaming the streets, rather than her ornament being broken. You could not win with her; if she had come back and seen the head off her ornament we would have regretted that much more!

It had to be the one of the strangest times of all my life. In less than a year we had left Leeds, lived by the sea, and lived in a cottage in a village that seemed to be in the middle of nowhere, but with every single move the ability to adapt was almost immediate.

If that constant figure, that was my mam, was near and present, nothing ever felt too daunting. My mam made things look easy and always made me feel secure, no matter what she was feeling. In some cases, I know she was scared and only because she told me years later.

The time finally came when my mam met someone. He was the complete bipolar opposite of my dad in all ways. He was six feet something, blond haired and red faced, just like a lobster. He spoke posh and I instantly disliked him. I mean that would always be the case even if he were a saint, he was not my dad but there was something more to this man.

I felt straight away he had a mean side. He was not wholesome, I could feel it, we all could feel it. He was putting on the act for my mam. Later down the line his true colours would become very apparent indeed.

The next move was imminent. Winter lets at the time came with a nine-month tenancy and that period was nearly up. My mam had found a three-bedroom semidetached house in a nearby town that she had bought (with the boyfriend) and we were to be on the move once again.

The fact she had bought it with him made me realise that he was a hard fixture now, and in my little mind I knew I had to find a way to get used to him. I knew also that it was not going to be easy, but that I had to make it work for me. I always knew that, always knew how to make things work for me, to be happy, as being sad did not make me feel good.

You have got to be happy in this life, my dad always used to say that to me!

Change is inevitable.

And it is not always kind.

Time will just keep ticking on by,

Never to rewind.

Be present. Be content.

Embrace every little moment.

For right here and now is all that is important,

The significance of now should always take prominence.

EIGHT

NEWTOWN

Things moved quickly as they always did with my mam. I loved our new house. It was light and spacious and as ever, my mam had it looking like a little palace. She really had an eye for style. Never tacky, always tasteful and above all, it was always homely!

One of her favourite sayings was "It's not where you live, it's how you live." It will always resonate with me. We were situated right in the heart of the town and after coming from the back and beyond, this was very much welcomed.

We were literally a stone's throw away from all the shops and even though it was a little town, there was so much more to see and do. Even better, it was right there, almost on our doorstep. It was roughly the start of July so there was no school now until the September. My mam had already enrolled us all, so we were just waiting.

Everything was changing but in the best way possible. My big brother was coming home! I was ecstatic. It was not wholly his choice though, and the surrounding factors were painfully sad. He really wanted to stay with my dad, but my dad was finding it hard to look after himself, let alone his 15-year-old son. Things that were going on had been passed back to my mam.

My dad, who by then was taxying, was living a bachelor's lifestyle, late night card games, gambling and heavy drinking. My brother had contracted scabies and even though this was a common thing, my mam could not abide this. He was not being looked after properly. My dad would not have done this to be purposefully neglectful, he just was not coping.

This was, in effect, the golden opportunity for my mam to take her son back. My mam promised my brother everything under the sun to entice him home (a new, top of the range stereo, I remember vividly, being the ultimate draw). Finally, he reluctantly relented!

He knew himself that it wasn't working. He was coming home to a home he did not know, and a place that was completely alien to him. My mam had us all back together though, and I could see the happiness shining like sunbeams through her eyes!

It was however, to be the last time I would see my dad until quite a few years later. He had become quite depressed by now, and understandably so. Losing my brother was the straw that broke the camel's back. My big brother had given him a purpose.

We had all got the train up to Leeds as usual, and my dad picked us up in his taxi from the station and took us to nannies. Over the following week whilst we were there, he would come and pick me and my little brother up and take us out. He was still funny and kind, but I could see the light had been switched off inside his daddy façade; he was truly broken!

I just felt so sorry for him, but what could I do? I just loved and hugged him so much more than I ever had before. After that visit, his father role relinquished. He hit rock bottom. The distance was too much for him, but primarily, he could not bear that another man had taken his place.

He would regret it years later. He told me so. I never felt betrayed by him though. Even as a young girl, I possessed empathy and understood why he did it. By now though I had already broken my heart over him once before, after him and my mam spilt up. I accepted the situation; I knew I had to.

I tucked him away into a special place in my heart.

Learning self-preservation from such a young age is imperative for mental health and even though I didn't know I was doing it at the time, that is precisely just what I was doing. I knew even then (not even being quite eleven years old) that is what I had to do.

I was taking care of my little heart and mind, and I had already started to take care of my little brother also. I knew he needed me, and in more ways than either of us both knew, at that time, just how much!

I was completely elated to have my big brother home, but I could also see how much he had grown and changed. He was four years older than me, and it showed. I could just tell he was different somehow. He was a hiding a sorrow that he wouldn't share with anyone, he would never do that. I knew though.

He had a pool of negative emotions, whirling around inside, and he had no idea what to do with them. His youthful spirit had taken a battering, and it was to be a while before the sadness and weariness, were to lift from his face. He did not want to leave my dad, that is all I knew.

He made friends fast, with the tough lot, the ones who had experienced hardship and pain, who travelled their own paths, the non-conformist, the rebels so to speak. They were nothing but courteous in our house, and respectful to say the least, my mam would not have tolerated anything other. It all started to iron out pretty quickly, and like us all, my big brother was not going to curl up in a ball, he was going to enjoy whatever life had in store for him.

He made ample use of his good looks and charm. The young ladies absolutely idolised him. He was to become a heartbreaker without even trying, but always the gentleman. I was proud to call him my brother. He was not just beautiful on the outside, but the inside too!

I had started my new school, which was just a stone's throw away, so I could walk there and back with my younger brother. It was difficult initially, as I had built my guard up so high, I found it hard to trust!

I had been to quite a few schools before this one, and each time there had been a negative experience. I presented myself as aloof and detached, but the children there were not like where I had come from. They were generally quite sweet!

I was not used to it. One wrong look from anyone in Leeds, meant a good right hook in the face, a punch in the throat. We were taught to hit first. I was ten years old!

I was very nasty to a girl who lived on the street and my mam caught me! She gave me another talking to and stated I would be a very lonely girl if I continued to be spiteful like that. I went down and apologised to my friend, and she basically told me the same! She had my card marked, and from that day on she held a special place in my heart. She spoke the truth.

Really all I wanted, was to make friends. I soon began making them, and it was there I met my best friend, who continues to be so now! She was one of the prettiest girls I had ever seen, blonde hair and blue eyes. She was kind and sweet and we had an instantaneous connection. I knew her immediately. She had the gift of knowing and understanding. She got me. She knew she did not have to feel threatened by me in any way. I was a truly sweet girl at heart. Sweet but tough, as my life had taught me to be. If I liked someone, I was fiercely loyal, and kind. She was the same. She was my kindred spirit and always will be. I love her with all my heart and feel lucky to have met her when I did. I believe she was sent to me.

My brother and I had started at the same school, him being in the year below, and our love hate relationship began to thrive. We had had at least three fights in the playground, and I mean full on punch ups. One time, I was playing jingle jangle, and he started to pull the elastic. I politely warned him once, but he did not want to stop, he was up for a fight.

This antagonist behaviour in him would always put me in a quandary. I knew I would humiliate him, and would usually give him two warnings to try and make him think about this (he was honoured). He wanted a scrap though, he knew the warnings and was up for it and therefore I could not disappoint him. All hell broke loose.

We were like a pair of wild animals; nobody could tear us apart. I eventually reigned supreme, by securing him in a headlock until he eventually succumbed. I was a kind fighter (had it been him he would have thrown in a couple of punches if he had me in the headlock).

My mam was called into the school for a meeting. They could not cope with us, and in all their time had never seen anything like it! It was a good job I was leaving for big school, as there was no doubt we would have been expelled otherwise.

We still had not mellowed in all of our ways, and were up to our usual tricks, of being downright naughty little shits. Our neighbour was an old lady who we deemed to be miserable and haughty, so we decided we would play a few of our games with her. This particular game, consisted of filling a water spray bottle up and when we would see her bedroom light come on at night; we would lean out of my bedroom window and spray, spray and spray! We did this repeatedly for a few consecutive nights until she finally realised what was going on and reported us to our mam.

My mam hit the roof once again, and we were simultaneously whacked hard around the head. I am thinking we must have liked being whacked because it never seemed to deter us. We just couldn t help but concede to that unruly little devil.

It turns out the old lady had lost her husband the year before and was in fact, terrified! That really affected me, and my brother also. We decided to go and apologise to the lady personally. My mam would never tell us what we should do. She would make us sit and think about what the right thing to do was.

The old lady was actually very lovely and so sweet. After our initial getting off on the wrong foot scenario, we all became good friends, and my brother and I started to do little errands for her to repay our mischievous deeds.

It was round this time, whilst living in this house, my mams best friend from Leeds, had decided to move down too. Her daughter was my best friend, we had grown up together, and now we were going to continue to do so. I was ecstatic. We were like sisters really. Ten days difference of age between us, and our sense of humour combined was like dynamite.

She was a stubborn girl and even though no fighter, she took no shit from me. One of the reasons I loved her, but her wicked humour was the main. We were indestructible together and just loved to laugh!

We were soon to become the Yorkshire terriers and had all and sundry eating out of the palms of our hands.

Teachers were called by their first names by us, fully accepted without them batting an eyelid, even the scariest ones let us off with everything. We had the wit and charm to get away with blue murder, and we honestly didn t have a care in the world. We bounced off each other effortlessly and so seamlessly. She was then and continues to be my best friend!

My sister had started at one of the local high schools but was going into the third year there (which I believe is year nine now). It was not easy at all for her, as everyone had already made their little friendship groups. She was like a fish out of water!

She had a broad Leeds accent and was small. We all were. She literally had to fight someone every day! She would not take any shit from no one and my sister, out of all of us, would beat someone senseless until they got the message!

They soon would get the message; she was savage, but again, my dad had instilled that so deeply into her that sometimes she did not know when to stop!

She hated it at the new school. My mam in some way or another had planted the seed in her head, that if she got kicked out then she would be going back to Leeds. That is all my sister wanted, she had left all her friends in Leeds and loved school there. She was a fantastic runner and was already winning medals for her cross-country abilities and was thriving there.

Anyway, she had concocted a plan to get expelled (already had her little bag packed for Leeds). Mission accomplished, but to her utter dismay, the whole school year felt it was an extreme injustice and decided to go on strike to get her back in!

Some had banners made, and others paraded placards with her name emblazoned, with words to the effect of, we want her back, let her back in! It whipped up quite a storm and the local paper printed the story. She became a local celebrity, but it was to be at her detriment.

She was devastated. The school let her back in. It was not for long though; she was eventually expelled.

None of the other local schools would have her (quite frankly they wouldn t touch her with a bargepole). My mam though, completely undeterred, got her into another school, in a different town. Authorities could not cope with her at all. In one of her school reports one of the teachers gave no other comment than "Who is this girl"?

I think we all wondered that about her at times. She was a living conundrum, but I do not think she was ever able to express her true feelings. Nobody ever really sat down and asked her what was actually wrong. Even if they did, I believe she felt she could not actually say. She was not good at articulating herself and this is why she was so angry.

My mam could not cope with it, her motto was just to get on with it. My mam just steamed on through everything, but at some point, that steaming on through catches up with you. Feelings were not discussed back then; you were left to figure out a lot on your own.

I believe the only person who ever really understood my sister, was my mams youngest sister, her and my sister had a very special bond, and I am grateful she at least had that.

I was beginning to like my new life away from Leeds, which I never thought would ever happen. My cousins would come to stay and one time, my cheeky, charismatic cousin had made his way down to see us. He must have been twelve at the time. He turned up on his own with a teddy for my mam (it had "I love you" written on the front of it).

He had driven near on three hundred miles, all on his own. He had nicked a car in Leeds and when he seen it was running out of petrol, he just pulled into a service station and nicked another. He stole three cars to get from Leeds to Devon. I know this is probably beyond anyone's comprehension to believe this, but it was true!

My mam was not angry with him at all, it just made her love him even more. She understood his life. He'd been running from the police for years, that wasn't going to change. The sentiment meant more to her than anything. He just missed her so much and just wanted to be with her.

I found out later that she wanted to adopt him when he was younger, but it never came to fruition for whatever reason. My mam kept that teddy, pride of place, on her dressing table, always.

It was always so exciting whenever my cousins came to visit, but again, everything had to be tarnished! I did not see colour when I looked at my family, I just saw love. They were no different to anyone else as far as I was concerned, but where I lived, I do not think many people had ever seen a person of mixed race.

I do not think many of the people had been out of Devon. I now know that these people were ignorant, small, minded people who had never educated themselves, or more importantly had never been educated to know any different.

Black people were still very second classed citizens to them, and the prejudice oozed from their mouths, and on more than one occasion, these comments were to be met by my fist! These people were my family and if you were going to speak about them in any ill way, there would be consequences.

I loved them so much, and as much as I loved them coming to visit, there was always that apprehension that went with it. It meant my guard would have to come back up to his maximum. I would not keep friends with any person who made even the slightest derogatory reference about a black person.

I went to a friend's house for tea one night after school. I met her mum for the first time, and she seemed really lovely. We sat down for tea and a Paul young song started playing. I absolutely loved him and exclaimed excitedly how I loved the song. The mum replied very sharply 'Really? He has wogs as his backing singers"!

I was utterly gobsmacked and speechless (which was probably a first for me). My friend was genuinely embarrassed and proclaimed loudly 'mum" to which then her mum became very defensive, with her pathetic reasoning of why. She just hated them, and that was simply it. No other explanation, no real reason, no justification as to why.

I said nothing. She was an adult, but I felt disgusted and vilified inside. I was not angry though, I felt extreme pity for her, but I knew there and then, that I would never set foot in her house again, and I told my friend exactly that. I had no malice towards my friend. She had not said it, but I knew we would never be the same again. I had to be extremely careful about who I was going to get close to, I had to be.

I loved my family so much, but it was so hard being part of a mixed-race family. My brothers and sister were white. They were not, but they were my blood, my cousins, my aunties, my mams sisters, nieces and nephews. They were my family, and I would fight for them no matter what. I had seen them suffer for it over the years, and it was so unfair and so unjust.

My protectiveness over them was so strong, but it was not easy by far. I just never understood how the colour of a person's skin could cause such hate and animosity. It completely perplexed me. We had been brought up around reggae music, Jamaican food and culture and it was just as much in my blood as it was theirs.

I knew from a very young age that being white gave me so much more privileges, and it made me feel extremely uncomfortable and awkward. I never felt better than them or lucky even, I felt sad, aggrieved and confused about it.

I felt empowered being part of such an amazing family. We were strong, diverse and incredibly open minded. Every single one of us were outstanding, in one way or another. I never felt superior in any way at all, but I knew I was different, because I was white. I just couldn t understand and never will, why the colour of a person's skin could perpetuate such hatred. I was proud of my family and my roots, and I always will be.

You learn over the years that you cannot fight everyone who is racist, you learn that not everyone has been as lucky as you to experience such diversity. Most people are just ignorant and have had the hatred instilled in them from their peers. There is good in bad in all walks of life, and I know I am not superior to any other because of the colour of my skin.

People in our small town were beginning to get to know us as family, and most people respected us, so the rest of my family were starting to be accepted. I look back now and believe we all educated quite a few people. I think even if certain people thought nasty things, they would not dare say them out loud as they knew they could not handle the repercussions.

My mam was working hard by this time, with three different jobs on the go. She was mostly always home at teatime cooking a satisfying meal for us all though; and this always gave me a warm, fuzzy feeling inside. This is another thing I apply in life.

She set a lot of examples but my, she had one hell of a temper and was not afraid to let it loose in the slightest. One particular teatime, she had cooked tea and the four of us were messing about at the table. She was in the kitchen at the time, but she was hearing what was going on! We were nicking each other's food and arguing over it.

The next minute, the table's been thrown in the air, food is flying everywhere, and all of us (except me, I was quite clever at dodging them, most of the time), simultaneously had been whacked hard around the head! Her speed and timing were phenomenal. So precise and exact, it must have only taken seconds.

Needless to say, we all went without tea (until later, when she called us down to finish it). You just could not mess with her!

We all had menial chores to do and if she were going to work, she would leave us notes. I felt embarrassed by the notes; because of her lack of education, her spelling was absolutely atrocious. Hoover was spelt Hovver, and any was spelt eny and she rarely spelt my name right.

I did not know much about her life at that time, and because I was so clever, I had her deemed as thick and stupid. I was embarrassed by her. I obviously feel ashamed of that now and it is now one of the things that make me love her more.

On one occasion I decided I could not be bothered to do my chores. I was fed up with being her slave (of course I was not her slave but when you are made to wash dishes at 11 you feel like it!).

My best friend (from Leeds) had come round to call for me, to go into town and we were all giddy to go. With that my mam walks in from work, she had seen the dishes were not done and straightaway, she was not happy!

I had a proper hiding for that, and not just a whack around the head (all in front of my friend). A well-known cartoon was on at the time and my friend just absorbed herself in that and was laughing away (she was used to it). My friend was then sent home, and I was sent up to my room for the rest of the day! I wasn t particularly bothered about the hiding. I was just fuming that my friend was laughing (even if the cartoon was funny).

I did not try that again though. My mam didn t give a damn about who was there. I should have known better. You would always get your lesson.

My mam was gaining quite the reputation from all of our friends as a woman you just could not mess with. She treated every single one of them as if they were her own, when they entered into our house.

There were two matching ornaments of horses which were situated at each end of the mantel piece in our dining room. They were lovely ornaments, my mams houses were always decorated and furnished to a high standard. The back door was where everyone came in and out of.

My eldest brother, by now, had settled in perfectly and it was like he had never been away. I loved having him around, as did my mam, but he had a lot of older friends and was up to things beyond his years. He was starting to flex his freedom a little too much for her liking. He was not living in a hotel she had stated and there were certain rules he had to follow. He wasn t adhering to these rules, and she had to make it clear to him.

There were a few occasions when he waltzed in completely oblivious to the fact that she had been worrying about his whereabouts and he would be met by one of those horse ornaments, flying straight into his direction. It 's like she could sense him coming because she would always be prepared for his entrance. It would have made no difference if he had company. It could have flown into them for all she cared. Her temper was lethal but captivating also.

One of my brothers' friends (who my mam loved and I did also) nicknamed that ornament 'The flying horse '. It would always get placed back onto the mantel piece after each incident in its usual pride of place.

It ended up without its tail, an ear, a leg and was covered in scratches, but it was always placed back there. It was a consistent reminder of the lesson you might receive if you dared to go against her wishes. That 'flying horse 'is still fondly remembered. I wish I had kept it as a trophy!

The boyfriend was starting to find his feet and his confidence was beginning to show. He was not finding it easy, living in our four shadows and he liked nothing more than more, than when my mam would lose her head on one of us, especially my sister!

The fair was in town, and my mam had asked my sister to take me with her. My sister did not want to take me, as she had her own plans, but she could not say no, so off we went. We had been given a time curfew of 9 o 'clock but my sister was having way too much of a fun time with her friends and some lads, and we got back later than we should have.

The boyfriend was already out looking for us. On seeing us, he motioned to my sister the finger slash across his neck (your dead) he had the most sinister smirk on his face, my blood ran cold. The minute we stepped through the door, I was greeted with an almighty whack around the head, and then sent up to bed.

My sister though, was given the worst hiding, starting from the front room into the dining room, whilst the boyfriend just stood there and watched with his arms folded! I screamed for my mam to stop, but he coldly pointed me back to my room. I was scared for my sister.

That day, I hated him more than I had ever hated anyone in my life. Any person with an ounce of compassion would have intervened and stopped that at once. Why would he even want my mam to get in such a state was beyond me. He fuelled the fire and watched the inferno spread, without a shred of emotion. He was sadistic and cold, and I kept that all to myself. There had to be another way to deal with him I just was not quite sure what!

I did however, tell my mam that she overstepped the line, and that if he was a decent man, he wouldn t have let that happen. She took it from me and knew exactly what I meant.

The dog was in his element, more than I had ever known him to be. He was off on his jollies all day long. He was streetwise and liked his freedom more than anything in the world. My mams attempts to discipline us into walking him would never succeed. You could take the dog out of Leeds, but you could never take Leeds out of that dog.

He chose us that dog, for no matter where we went, and with his ample freedom, he always came home. He was still my dog though, and my mam would tell me this, for whenever I was on my way home, he was at the door wanting to be let out, and he would always meet me on my way home. That dog understood timing and had an amazing instinct. I loved him so much.

I was now in secondary school and loved it. Even though because of my sister eventually being expelled and by now my eldest brother had (both for fighting). The teachers assumed I would follow suit.

This literally devastated me, but my mam asked them to put me on report for a month (which devastated me even more). Her view was that they would soon see how different I was, and she was right.

They could not believe it, now not that I was not averse to a scrap or two but my thirst for learning totally outweighed that. It was not long before I had every single teacher eating out of the palm of my hand and not that much longer after, when we were all on a first name basis!

It was easy for me as I was naturally bright and loved to learn. I liked to show off a bit also and was quite a big head. I had a lovely singing voice and would sing from morning till night if I could. I was settled inside and felt as free as a bird.

Nobody would even attempt to bully me, mostly because of my sister. She may not have shown her love in a demonstrative way, but made it very clear, you did not go near me. I felt like I ruled the world, and it was the happiest I had felt in a long time.

Life was good, and we were to be on the move again. This move was like no other move before. I was not being uprooted to another world or moon. We were simply relocating to a different part of town. Out of the town and into a newer house.

My mam was moving upmarket!

Oh, the stars are displaying their twinkling in magnitude,

They are exquisitely just curtseying to me tonight.

Just for me they are shining.

I am joyous and beguiling and righteous for this sight.

I am dancing with them for I am on the moon.

My heart is made of a million stars.

For now,

I am the light.

NINE

UPMARKET

I was rather annoyed about this move to be honest. It would cause me too much inconvenience; I would have to catch the bus! I was becoming quite the little madam, and it was grating on my mam's nerves. She soon gave me a good talking to though, and I was thoroughly put back in my place.

I was told no one likes a big head or a know it all. She could not care less if I could sing or not, or how clever I was at school. I was no better than anyone else in our household.

If I thought anyone was going to bow down to me, I was very much mistaken. I had to get off my high horse, or else! My legs were made for walking, there was such a thing as a bus, and to be quite frank, she could not give a shit what I thought!

The thing is, she did, she cared what we all thought, but I was the only one who ever dared say anything, and it absolutely fumed her! She would make sure she did not show it though, and her way was to tell me that she did not give a shit, and to put me well and truly back in order!

Even though I assumed I was way cleverer than her, she would soon make me feel otherwise. You did not mess with her, and if you did it would be at your peril. After a large serving of humble pie, I would soon pipe back down, there was only so far you could go with her, as I knew very well if I were to push anymore, her next trick would be the notorious, mighty whack around the head! Once my mam had made her mind up, that was that!

Life was heading in the right direction by now. We had a lovely house with a beautiful garden where my mam was in her element. It even had a palm tree; we thought they only grew abroad. My mam spent hours in that garden, planting and pruning. She was naturally green fingered.

My nanny especially loved that house, and the palm tree. She would tell anyone who would listen back up north, how we had a palm tree in our garden, and she would tease us all that we were posh! It was a three-bedroom semi-detached house on an estate which just had to have a palm tree in the garden! It still makes me laugh today.

My eldest brother had started work now and had grown into a man. My mam had made sure of it. If he was not going to continue in school, then he was to get a job, and start to pay his way in life! I suppose that was fair, and the way it went, but it all seemed to be happening so quickly.

He was still as lovely as ever to me and I would run around after him, making him cups of tea and doing his packed lunch up for him. I would do absolutely anything for him. He in return would take me to the local discos, and most weeks when he got his pay packet, would treat me, by taking me into town, and letting me pick something I wanted. Usually this was a poster for my room or some type of stationery. He was always treating me. I loved it of course, I felt so lucky having this wonderful big brother that nobody else had, he was very much like a dad in many ways, and extremely protective over me. He was popular, hilariously funny and so good looking, and all the girls fancied him.

If he ever liked a girl, he would tell them that they had to meet me first, and if I did not like them, it was a no go. I think this made him even more desirable as let's face it, there is nothing more attractive than a man who loves his mam and his little sister. He had good taste in the girls though, and I think I can only remember one time, when I did not take to one of his girlfriends, but that was to be much later in life!

My sister pretty much lived in a world of her own world. My mam had nicknamed her dolly daydream, and to be honest, I think she used it as a coping mechanism. She was often criticised and put down for her lack of conforming.

She hated school and had no desire in any subject so would often spend her time skiving (playing truant) and she loved the attention of the opposite sex. Why not? She was beautiful looking with thick, dark brown hair and the biggest brown eyes! She knew how to work it, and could have the pick of any man, but would become bored extremely fast, or fall head over heels with the bad boy!

She loved fashion and every outfit down to the earrings had to match. She always looked immaculate but her and my mam would clash, and my mams temper would usually end up running through her fists! I hated that. There had to be a better way than that, I knew that.

Afterwards my mam would be in despair of herself, and I would usually end up consoling her and telling her that was not the way. My mams boyfriend relished in it though. He took great satisfaction in seeing one of us get a hiding, but more often than not, it was my sister who would get it. He was always behind the scenes stirring my mam into action. He would not try and defuse it, like any decent man would. He liked to escalate it to its highest heights, so my mam would lose her shit. I could see this and would tell my mam so. She would agree with me, and probably somewhere inside of her, would resolve to never repeat it. Even though it became less frequent, it was also somehow acceptable. My sister was not easy by far, but she never deserved that!

My sister and I were complete opposites. I was only interested in school, and I know I irritated the hell out her; she did not understand me, nor I her. I was not interested in boys. I fancied boys, but I was more interested in myself to be honest. I can see why I could be deemed as selfish, but I had a vision for my future, and everything else seemed petty and irrelevant. I was way too logical about things, whilst my sister was way too emotional about things and that aggravated me badly!

Sometimes, she would try and talk to me about these emotional things, and I would just cut her off with a deadpan look on my face or just bury my head into a book. I had no time for it. Then her emotions would kick in and she would fly for me, and then my logic would kick in, and I would run like lighting to my mam. My mam would proclaim with sincere justification that if anyone did the hitting in the house, it was her and only her! That is how most of the squabbles were dispelled in our house.

You would never hear that nowadays. It was fully accepted that our mam could punish us with a hiding. Even though she did go too far at times, a good old whack generally did the trick and seemed fair most of the time.

My mams boyfriend had started to find his place within are household and was increasing with confidence. One evening, my big brother had come home later than usual. My mam was in the front room and on this particular night and was having a few glasses of wine (which she rarely ever did). There was a new film out on video and my mam had mentioned to my brother that she had bought it. "I ll watch it in a bit" he said. With that the boyfriend piped up 'No you won t, because I m watching the news." My brother did not want to cause a problem and walked off, my mam on the other hand had seen something she did not like, and all hell broke loose!

My mam hit the boyfriend around the head with the wine bottle. He then, in return, grabbed hold of my mams hands and pulled her out of the room, then shoved her out of the front door. My brother had seen this happening and then ran out and started attacking him.

This was all going on in our front garden, right by the palm tree. I was utterly shocked, mortified and horrified. I had never seen my mam and boyfriend argue before and now this! The boyfriend was no fighter even though his six foot frame dwarfed my brother; my brother was throwing punches left, right and center.

My mam managed to get in the middle of them and diffuse it. It was all over in a minute or so, but it felt like a lifetime. I just stood there crying, just when I thought life was going well, it seemed like the world was crumbling around me. It was embarrassing more than anything for me.

I just hated drama, and this was one hell of a spectacle for the street to see, because that is what you think, you think that every other person and it 's dog sees everything what is going on, but in reality, they don 't!

I felt bad for my brother more than anything, he was just trying to do the dutiful thing and protect his mam. If the boyfriend weren 't such a nasty piece of work in the first place, it wouldn 't have happened. I think it just brought everything to boiling point!

I ran to my bedroom and flung myself on my bed, continuing to sob (very dramatically as well). With that the boyfriend came in. He was so full of apologies and remorse, but I think that was more to do with the fact that my brother had given him a hiding and it had frightened him. I know he never intended to hurt my mam. When drink is involved, things do become distorted and irrational. It was, I suppose, just one of those things.

My loyalties were only with my brother. Afterwards, I went into see my brother. He was sat on his bed with his head in his hands crying. The first time I had seen him cry. I put my arm around him and told him it was not his fault. He told me he loved me for the first time, and I told him I loved him back. It was an emotional night, but in hindsight it did buck everybody up, and the next day everyone was especially nice to each other.

I felt sorry for my mam. I wondered what the hell she was doing with the boyfriend, he behaved worse than us kids at times and his competitiveness served dramatic repercussions.

Things resumed back to normal quite quickly. My mam did not dwell on things and as far as she was concerned, grudges solved nothing. However, it never left me and my reservations about the boyfriend intensified even more.

Despite this, though, I knew being on the receiving end of the hiding from my brother would force him to change his tactics. I had to lock away my thoughts in one of my little compartmentalised boxes in my little head!

My youngest brother and I were still up for our thrills, and our latest was when my mam and the boyfriend went out. The telephone became our naughty tool. We would each take it in turns to dial a random number and create a saga of some sort. We liked particularly best to pretend we were Cilla Black and shout "Surprise, Surprise. It's Cilla here" down the line.

We were both good at imitating accents and had an absolute ball. Some people would actually fall for it (quite lot in fact!). We would be in stitches rolling around. It was hysterically funny, but as usual we crossed the line when I obtained some of the phone numbers of teachers at our school.

It was all going swimmingly, until we rang the deputy head mistresses' number and thought it would be a great idea to impersonate her (I was absolutely brilliant at imitating her). She was a Northern Ireland lady and just knew things! I was not as clever as I thought I was, as she had remembered my mimicking voice from a few weeks earlier at school.

I had a little run in with her one day and thought it was highly amusing to copy everything she said to me right back at her in voice! Of course, teachers talked in staff rooms, and they were becoming both annoyed and intrigued as to who were the phantom callers!

The cat was out of the bag and once again my mam was very much bemused and disappointed! Yes, we had a whack but if I am truthfully honest, it was always worth it!

The dog again, just went about doing his own thing. He was remarkably familiar now with his surroundings, but we were out of town. This was no deterrent for him at all. He would walk himself into town each day, through the subways and on the path he would go. It must have been a mile and half. Some of the kids I knew from where I lived would comment that they had seen him in the subway or walked with him a bit on the way. It was just the dog he was, and everyone talked about him like it was just a normal, everyday occurrence.

I didn't know any other dog who just did what it wanted, and even though people may have thought it was wrong, nobody ever said anything. I don't think they would have dared. Everyone knew that dog, and everyone thought a lot of him. One of the lads from the estate commented one day to me, that when people say their dogs look their owners, our dog was the image of us four, and he was!

He would follow me everywhere, and I would have to turn around and tell him sternly to go home. He would then turn around, and I would watch him disappear around a corner, only to find him following me again. I could never be mad at him for long.

My mam said she would always know what bus I would be on. There was a 4.10 that would arrive at the bus stop at 4.25 and a 4.40 that would arrive at 4.55. She knew I would not be on the earlier bus as he would just lie in his basket and if I were the on the later bus, he would be scratching at the door so to come and meet me and vice versa.

If I was on the earlier bus. He would be sat at the end of the lane waiting for me as if to say, I am walking you back now, and I just loved seeing his little proud, handsome face. He really was extraordinary and a proper little character!

I was excelling at school in every subject, and I was in top group for most of my lessons. My reports were mostly A's and B's, and my mam would tease me that I was the postman's. I know though, if she had any education herself, she would have been the same!

We were still in frequent contact with our Leeds family and would go up as often as possible. My mam never used to tell my nanny that we were visiting so to surprise her. We would catch the train up and get a taxi to nanny's house.

We always knew she would be in as she rarely left her house and would spend her days sat around her round table in the kitchen doing jigsaw puzzles, crosswords or reading books, whilst drinking endless cups of tea and smoking super king after super king. When the evening came, her special brews would then replace the tea.

We would be quiet as mice and my mam would send one of us in to poke our head around the door. The excitement was like no other. My nanny would look up and see one of our little faces and literally just start crying with emotion! It would set us all off, then after a few minutes she would being calling us all bastards, fuckers and cunts, all spoken with pure love!

I absolutely loved going back home and seeing my family. We would sleep wherever there was a space, and it was like we had never been away. I had become extremely adaptable by now, and even though I was only 13 years old, I was strong and resilient.

It was almost like I was being prepared for what lied ahead.

I will be kind to myself.

I will be happy, and the universe will conspire with me.

I know this.

I am lucky for I have love and essentially,

It is all that I need.

I am blessed immeasurably.

TEN

THE DIAGNOSIS

There was something in the air, but I could not quite put my finger on it! My mam was behaving differently, she was almost serene, unruffled and absent in her presence. She was contemplative, and I had never seen this in my mam before. I felt uneasy and knew something was going on, but my mam was a master at keeping her cards close to her chest.

My intuition was screaming at me. When I asked my mam what was going on she was cunningly dismissive and jumped right back into herself. It was nothing and everything was fine. I scrutinised her face closely for any sign of untruth, however she managed to pacify the nagging irritation in my gut.

A few days later, my mam dropped the news that we were moving. When I found out where it was, I dissolved into the queen of all meltdowns. We were moving to an estate, a council estate. I just could not fathom this out. Why? It was like we were going backwards. I did not understand. I thought we were on the up. This may sound shallow, I know, but my experiences with council estates were of fighting and being on your guard. I liked my house here and I did not want to live on a council estate. I liked my life here.

My mam explained it was a lovely house and she would have it like the one we were in, if not better. It did not matter where we lived but how we lived! It did not matter what I had to say it was final and as always, I would just have to accept it. Like it or lump it! I lumped it alright; but I was downright distraught and thoroughly miserable about the whole scenario!

We moved into our new house and just like she promised it was beautiful inside. The whole house was done out from the top to the bottom. Her taste in décor was undeniably like no other. She had an eye for the tiniest detail. The settee was of the highest quality and luxurious. Our bathroom was opaquely tiled in soft beige. The carpets were of the best quality and fitted with underlay.

The house inside had a feeling of home, but we were still living on a council estate and people had judgements about council house dwellers. That is the part I did not like; for someone who had come from nothing, I sure as hell didn t behave like it.

She had the garden all done and we had a drive done at the front with wooden gates. She planted flowers, plants, shrubs and made it look lovely. For the following March, she planted all the spring bulbs. I was fourteen though, and none of that mattered to me. I did not want to live on that estate.

I was undoubtedly a snob (which is laughable in itself, considering where we came from). I thought I knew everything and what everybody thought. The others were not like me, they never contested my mam. I would roll my eyes at her and openly disapprove at something I did not like. By then if she would go to clout me, I would move away and tell her very assertively that she was not going do it.

I was morally very right, and my mam found it hard to argue with me. On the other hand, I never gave her a reason to worry about me in any way, so I made it easy for her in that respect!

As per usual, I adapted quickly. I made friends with a few people on the street and was always one step ahead of the game. My life skills had taught me to see an event unfold way before any others could. My mind was quick, as were my actions. I was at the top at school and our move never wavered that.

By this time, I had a good handful of friends. I was popular, smart and still singing. My friends from school were playing a big part in my life. I would go to their houses for tea, and they evidently wanted to come to mine. I could not hold the inevitable off much longer. They would have to see where I lived. Nobody cared about where I lived, just me.

My mam was a fantastic cook and was not into instant food. She liked to cook everything from scratch. She could turn a roast chicken into a curry, a rice dish and a soup for consecutive days. Only once a week we were allowed what she called 'Crap Food," turkey burgers, frozen pizza, chips etc. Whenever I invited a friend over, I would have to find out what they liked to eat, and she would cook it.

My mam would sing and perform much to my discomfort, but every friend would tell me they wished they had a mam like mine, and I loved it. She got each and every one of my friends; and it did not matter what background they came from; they loved coming to my house. Everyone liked to be around my mam, she was funny and kind, and of course, secretly I liked it. She embarrassed me to a credit, never as a cringe. She to me was an incredibly special mam.

The boyfriend was becoming more demanding it seemed. He was a petulant, stroppy boy in a man's disguise. He liked to get his own way by stamping his feet, yes really! He was in competition with all of us. He was a big overgrown, spoilt baby and he would fend for attention from my mam, like a baby bird, flapping his wings for worms.

I had little respect for him, as did my brothers and sister. He was pathetic, week and insipid and he knew we thought this. It was overtly obvious. He had no backbone and he craved sympathy; his life had become an injustice because he could not have my mam all to himself.

He had his own cupboard in the kitchen with a lock on it, filled with all of his special treats. He loved sweets and would sit with a bag in his hands all scrunched up and held closely to his chest in case any of us decided to pounce. If you were really lucky, he would offer one to you, but I would always refuse out of sheer stubbornness and principle. I could not give a fuck about his manky sweets, and even if I wanted one, I would never have given him the satisfaction of letting him know. He was stingy and selfish to the maximum. It was almost like he could not bear to see us eat, that might mean we would survive. He was the absolute epitome of greed!

He hid things that my mam had bought for us that we liked, such as peanut butter. My eldest brother had come home one evening and was making toast, he was looking for the peanut butter and my mam had gone in the kitchen to help him look for it. She had only just bought it that day as she knew my brother liked it. They searched all in the cupboards but to no avail. My mam was bugged at this as she knew exactly where she had put it. It was a mystery.

I though, previously that evening, had seen the boyfriend put it into his locked cupboard. It made me feel sick and I just blurted out 'Did you not put that in your cupboard earlier?" in front of everyone. His face went crimson, and he stared at me as if to say 'Shut the fuck up, you little bitch" I was not having any of it and told him I had seen him do it. He did not want to go again with me and changed his tactic; by this time, he knew his game was up and proceeded to his cupboard to retrieve the peanut butter, whilst making pitiful excuses. It was embarrassing for him.

My poor mam looked crestfallen. My brother winked at me and continued to have his peanut butter on toast exclaiming how good it tasted in the process. I was laughing at his performance and the revenge was sweet. My mam later hit the roof with him and as always, he would flounce out of the house.

His calculated victories would always backfire on him. I still would have never conceived at that time though just how low he could actually go!

By this time, me and my mam were getting to a stage where we would talk about things and there were more times than not, I felt equal to her with my understanding. She respected my opinions, and for a while now, was asking me them. I would not just have just given them to her without her asking, she wouldn't have taken that, but we were growing together.

She told me that I had been here before, that my knowing and honesty were something she had not really seen in a lot of people and that was something coming from her. Her truth was like nothing I have experienced in life. She would look me straight in the eye with the deepest sincerity and tell me those truths.

She told me that my self-worth was more precious than anything in this world and no matter what, no one could ever take that from me. No money on this planet could ever match the truth and that I was never to compromise my self-worth for anything or anyone. Her truth told me that I was special, and I believed everything she said.

My mam saw deep into people's souls.

My mam had started complaining of a bad back and eventually she booked herself into the doctors. The doctor was not concerned at all. She was thirty-eight young and fit. He sent her away with pain killers and she was basically told it would get better. My mam never complained about anything, and it started to niggle at me.

I was in town one day. She did not see me and was over the other side of the road. She was hunched over like an old lady, walking very slowly, whilst rubbing her back. My instinct was screaming at me to run over but my head was telling me no! I did not like seeing it and wanted to pretend I had not. If she knew I was over the road, she would have straightened herself up immediately.

There was something wrong. I had never seen my mam ill and something inside was telling me she was poorly and that it was much more than a bad back.

Later that day when I got home, she was sat by the fire, again rubbing her back. I hated seeing her vulnerable and shouted at her to go back to the doctors. For once in my life, she did not tell me off for shouting. I really knew then, something profoundly serious was going on and it took me back to just before the house move when I had sensed something way more sinister. I knew in my heart that there was way more to this.

My fifteenth birthday was approaching, and I had arranged to go to a disco with my friends. As always, we had a wonderful time. There was, as usual, a load of laughing and mucking around, as teenage girls do. A bus was picking us up and dropping us off in town. I remember walking back home from town feeling contented and happy, loving my friends and my life.

I was totally unprepared for the sight that was to greet me as I approached my home. An ambulance was parked outside, and I just ran as fast I could to my house. My mam was being wheeled out of the house on a stretcher. It was just terrible to see but even though I was panic stricken inside I managed to remain calm.

The words 'haemorrhaging fast echoed through my ears. My mam was as white as a sheet and lifeless. I was utterly petrified inside. I went into auto pilot. The boyfriend was screaming and was blubbering his eyes out. I shouted at him to stop, shut the fuck up and calm down!

It seemed to work as he just went quiet. I knew there and then that I had to keep strong whilst everything around me dissolved into sheer chaos. I had to stay focused for my mam. She was rushed into hospital, sirens blaring!!

Even though it sounds stupid, I did not like the idea of being the subject of the neighbour's gossip and I felt agitated by the whole episode; it seemed like every person on the street were all stood outside watching the whole commotion. I just wanted to scream at the top of my lungs for them to all fuck off back into their houses. I expect most of them were actually concerned, but it felt like they all had tickets to the circus, and we were the main act!

I was told the next day she had to have a transfusion of five pints of blood and that she nearly died. My little heart was shattering inside, but I never wavered, I just could not, my mam would not have liked that!

I turned fifteen whilst she was in hospital. She had already wrapped my presents, but she was not there to see me open them. It was bittersweet really; she had bought me the fanciest hair dryer with a diffuser and loads of other bits I asked for, but all I wanted was my mam back home and for her to better. I learnt that day that materials meant nothing.

All I wanted was my mam!

My eldest brother by this time was working away in London. Nothing was being made into a big deal, even though we know inside it was. Our family was not like that, we were taught to just get on with it.

I remember my brother ringing one day and him asking me what I thought. I told him that he should not worry, and it was just a blip, that she was going to be okay, but it was the complete opposite of what I actually thought.

The truth is, in my heart I knew she was going die. I just knew it. I remember sitting in a classroom one day when I was about twelve years old, and my mind just wandered off whilst staring out of a window.

For some reason I had a clear vision of her dying within the next few years. Just at that moment, a crow came and perched on the window, right beside me. It was an omen, and I never shook that experience off. I was to have many more of them through my life and they always came true!

My youngest brother was always my biggest concern. He was lost. My mam was so protective over him, he was her baby. He was beside himself with worry and when I could, I would try and lift him up and help him feel a bit lighter. The dimensions in our sibling relationships were starting to change and by now our bonds were becoming much stronger.

My sister was completely disinterested and detached from me, and in a way, I resented her. She was my big sister, but she was so indifferent towards me. We just did not understand one another at all back then. I realise now that was her way of coping and she could barely look after her own emotional state, let alone extend herself to me. She internalised a lot my sister, and lacked confidence, she was always the problematic one and her voice was rarely heard. She was very misunderstood.

It was blatantly obvious that something dreadful was going on with my mam and I wanted answers. It is not nice being left in the dark when something is so obviously wrong.

I was eventually told she had the C word. CANCER!!!
Just like that, the world fell out of my bottom!

I am not looking for inspiration.

I am confounded within the walls of guilt, self-pity,

And total absorption of what ifs.

Wallowing entirely in this wretched, desolate abyss.

Anger is to be my one and only conquest.

Paltry meagre tears just will not suffice this.

I am utterly broken.

I am bereft.

ELEVEN

MAM COMING HOME

The transfusion was successful, and my mam was coming home! The euphoria was magical. The house just was not a home without her, it was miserable, sombre, dark and gloomy, my beautiful mam lit up my whole world. My mam arrived back to our home full of smiles and love. I was ecstatic. My mam was back, and life could resume back to normal.

She started making plans and was adamant she would be back to tip top health in no time. My mams optimism was contagious. It was all going to be ok.

She was a master of deception though and I found this out whilst carrying out my favourite past time, ear wigging!

The phone rang one evening and I sort of knew it was my aunty, her younger sister. The phone in those days was situated in the porch. It was placed on a table which also had a seat. The phones were plugged into the wall back then and you could not walk around with them.

It was always a long phone call with those two. It started off all chirpy and the laughing seemed to go on forever. I knew very well by my ear wigging experiences that once the hushed tones applied; it was about to get down to the nitty gritty. I was gripped now as I could sense it was becoming juicy, but my god, if there was a time that I wished I had minded my own business it was then. My mam obviously assumed the coast was clear.

I stood rigid on the landing, my little heart pounding loudly in my abbreviated, shallow chest, and then came the bombshell. My mam whispered that the cancer could possibly be terminal. They wanted to start chemotherapy! They would see how the radiotherapy went and take it from there. She was worried about losing her hair and was feeling frightened of the prospect.

That was enough for me to comprehend in one hit, and I gently tiptoed back into my room. I flung myself onto my bed being careful as for not wanting to cause attention to myself. I cried my little heart out.

My mam came up a little while later to see if I was ok. She could see I had been crying and wanted to get to the bottom of it but like her I was also becoming a master at holding my cards close to my chest and told her that I had just read a sad extract from one of Jane Eyre's novels. She accepted that as she knew how passionate I was about English Literature.

We had a cuddle and both of us seemed to hold on for that little longer than any other time before. I did not want to let her go, not this time and not ever. The melancholy echoed through the whole of my entire and wanted to explode out of me right there and then.

I just could not bear the thought of being without the one person who was the universe to me, and my troubled little soul was praying for a miracle.

I also knew I could not tell a soul, my brothers and my sister most definitely not, it would cause sheer panic and pandemonium and I knew my mam couldn't have dealt with that.

The burden felt colossal, but I also knew that once it was out in the open, it would become real. I had to have faith and hope and I also reverted to the fact that my mam at times could be quite the drama queen. It was all part of my coping mechanism.

My mam and the boyfriend had decided to go on holiday. They chose the Algarve. My mam's first ever time abroad. I felt she deserved it and even though I knew I would miss her I also knew in my heart she needed a break away. The sun might just possibly cure her perhaps. When you are fifteen you see the solutions to problems in the most absurd way and I always tried to understand the bigger picture.

My mam rang every day whilst she was on her holiday, and it was very apparent she was missing us all. I would say we were all fine. I wanted her to enjoy her holiday and was protective over her. I had seen her at her worst (or so I thought) and because of this I loved to see and hear her at her best.

I was a coper and even though I found things hard there was always an angelic intervention that would keep me calm, grounded and capable. No matter what was going on I always knew that no matter what, everything would be alright, it had to be, what was the point in living otherwise. I could turn everything around to make myself feel better. I did not like feeling sad, I mean who does?

She was home before we knew it.

She was tanned and looked the healthiest I had seen her for months and again in my little head I believed the sun had saved her and she was going to live, and everything was going to great. She absolutely loved it!

She missed us all incredibly and was planning the next holiday already but next time it would be with us all. I loved my bangle she had brought back for me. It was me down to T and I still have it until this day. I had missed her so much and was in my element to have her home.

My whole aspect on life was changing dramatically. I had gone from a young girl, having crushes on boys and worrying what I looked like to not giving an absolute damn. I just could not have cared less anymore, everything else became superficial!

All I cared was that my mam would get better. I had changed so much by now and was starting to become a much less selfish, kinder and a more understanding individual.

By this time Christmas was approaching. My mam loved Christmas and always made our Christmas special. It was the time of year when we would have everything we wanted. She loved to see us happy and always went that extra mile, even at times when I know money was tight for her, there was never a price at Christmas, and she would do what she had to do to see our little faces sparkle.

My mam pulled out all the stops for this Christmas. I had a new hairdryer (again), clothes and loads of other girlie bits, plus she gave me two hundred pounds. That was a lot of money back then and I was thrilled. I was always careful with my money, so I put some away and treated myself to a few little luxuries.

This was to be our last Christmas together and she knew it and in my little heart I did also. I was adamant on spending as much of my time as possible with her.

I wanted to know everything about her, and she reciprocated with an open heart. She was softer and warmer, and we held hands a lot. Something we would never normally do. She started to look me in the eye so meaningfully that it felt like she was transporting power into me (I know now that she actually was). She was taking time to infiltrate her mother's wisdom into me, and I took the time to absorb it as greedily as I could.

I was fifteen and I was set to live my life without my mam and even though those words were not exchanged it was so apparently obvious.

Her back was playing her up more than ever now, and even though I hate to say it, I could not bear to witness her in pain. It made the whole cancer thing more prominent, and I did not want to acknowledge the cancer at all. I was, even though accepting, paradoxically in denial.

The boyfriend had consumed the latest pioneer stacking deck, the latest form of art in stereo music. It was grand and the technology to it was quite intricate.

One night I had been out and when I got home my mam was sat in the darkness with the headphones on. She wanted to listen to some music but could not work out how to use it. She asked me to help her. It was like a red mist descended down on me. "You should be able to fucking do that" I shouted, "you can sort anything out" I continued, "just do it and be my mam"!

I ran up the stairs willing her to come up after me and whack me around the head! She did not because she could not and instantly my resolve weakened. I hated myself for it and cried myself to sleep that night.

I found it so hard to see her weak. Even though there was this huge understanding instilled in me, she was still my mam, and I was still her little girl, and the little girl wanted her strong, robust, super mam back. It was one of the biggest regrets of my life for a long time that my stupid stubbornness and self-pity did not repent. I should have gone back downstairs and helped her. This memory still breaks my heart.

The next day my mam eased my conscience by telling me my eldest brother had helped her, she wasn't sarcastic or trying to make me feel bad, she put both of her hands on my face and told me she understood and when I started to cry she wiped the tears away and exclaimed 'It would have bloody pissed me right off if some daft twat was dithering in the same way". I just cracked up laughing as did she!

I just loved her for that and becoming a mam myself helped me heal a lot of the guilt I had carried over the years. As a mam you understand your children and why they do the things they do but it is something only a mam can recognise.

We were into January now and her condition seemed to be deteriorating and it was becoming very apparent. She was still on top of the housework and keeping up appearances, but she had started to slow down, my mam usually did everything at top speed.

There was never any sombreness from her though and she never moaned, grumbled or complained. She absolutely detested self-pity and she did not like to be a hypocrite so feeling sorry for herself was most definitely off her agenda. She remained upbeat and positive as always.

She had started to open up to me about her life, hence the reason I learnt so much about her. We would sit for hours and talk and to be honest by now that is all I wanted to do with her. She would be soon to start chemotherapy and even though she may have thought about death she believed she would get better so it was never discussed, and she would have never of put that on me anyway.

She was forever showing me the way and how to behave in the hardest of situations. She was inspirational to say the least. I was in awe of her and her ability to appear so steady and calm when it must have been absolute hell for her. I still had never seen my mam cry or be scared.

I had gone to school one day as normal. Even when I was at school though, my thoughts always seemed to be with her. The worry inside me was all consuming but I would never show anything outwardly, it just was not me. I had to keep being strong. Looking back, it was an extreme amount of pressure to be shouldering at the young age of 15 but it was the only way I knew how to cope.

I was sat in my maths class just gazing out of the window when the door opened and in walked the deputy head. She started speaking in hushed tones to my maths teacher. My stomach knotted. My intuition was speaking to me, and it was telling me it was about my mam. I was right.

I was called out of class into the office, but I was not waiting to be sat down. I wanted to know there and then. My house was just up the road from my school and my little legs were getting ready to run.

The teacher wanted to do it all proper, by sitting me down in the office. I already felt all eyes on me and hated the melodramatic attention diverted towards me. "Just tell me now" I shouted but she was trying to calm me down, well that was not going to work.

My anger erupted and I broke free, whilst my little legs accelerated as fast as they could all the way up to my house. My mind was racing, I had already convinced myself that she had died on that short run home, and I was absolutely petrified. I was there in minutes to find the boyfriend sobbing profusely.

I consoled him, whilst he explained through his spluttered sobs that my mam had been rushed back into hospital after haemorrhaging again. To me though it was a relief, she was not dead, she had come out of hospital the last time after haemorrhaging, there was still hope and I told the boyfriend that. He was utterly beside himself and I was annoyed at that. It did not make me feel good at all and I told him he had to pull himself together. We had to be strong for each other.

To be honest as hard as it sounds, I just found him pathetic and insipid and it infuriated me that my mam had to deal with him, because I knew she got to see that from him too and probably a lot more.

I was always kind to him though out of all of us though, I felt sorry for him and even though I never understood what my mam saw in him but out of respect for her I felt I owed it to her to give him a chance. I was the one he let know what had happened that day and it was me that had to break the news to the rest of the family.

It was now the beginning of February. It was cold, dark and morose and it reflected my thoughts entirely. I was tired, bewildered and felt so scared. The one person who could make it better was not here to console me and not that she would have done anything, her presence was all that was ever needed. My security blanket was disintegrating, and I had to cling onto the hope that she could still make it through.

Hope, such a small, unassuming word, but what an incredibly powerful insight it offers when you feel you have nothing left!

The stars are still shining, and the moon is still as enticing.

Could they not just keep me to them and let me keep smiling?

The world will not stop turning just for my sadness.

Why are we falling into this terrifying darkness.

Nothing seems real and all that once was,

Means nothing at all,

We are all now just lost.

Of all of the people,

In all of this world,

Why my mam,

Please tell me why her?

TWELVE

HOSPITAL

I arrived at the hospital full of trepidation. I had no idea what to expect. I had seen films about people being poorly in hospital and expected my mam to be completely out of it and to be hooked up to a load of machines. She was sat upright looking as pretty as a picture, all made up and eating grapes. All of my anxiousness dissipated immediately.

She was her usual jovial self and beckoned me to sit by her. She explained that the radiotherapy was not working, and they were keeping her in to start the chemo. This satisfied me to a degree, but I had become quite sceptical and mistrusting. I had this niggling feeling in my gut, whispering (if not screaming) that she was lying.

I decided to confront her about his. I needed to know. I was mature enough to deal with these things now. I had been through enough in my life and she needed to know I could handle it. My mam assured me face to face that she was not hiding anything, and I believed her. She was so proud of me and that is exactly what I wanted her to be. Everything I had ever done was to make her proud of me. I was so protective over her wellbeing, and she knew that. She spoke candidly about the next stages and was as always ultra-upbeat and optimistic. Her main aim was to get better for us all and her determination was blatant for all to see. I was so proud she was my mam and I just loved her so much.

Things were becoming increasingly difficult at home. The boyfriend was not coping at all, and it was all about him. He could not think bigger than his hurt and we weren t a consideration. There was no food in the cupboards and whilst he was filling his stomach with Kentucky 's (I knew this as whenever he took me to the hospital, the empty boxes were piling up in his car.) My little brother and I were acting on our wits and survival.

There was a little shop at the bottom of our road and the owners were just lovely people. Usually there was no chance in the world I would ever ask any one for anything. We had all been brought up with pride and self-respect. In this case though, I took it on myself to ask for tick from the shop. I had already gaged they were lovely people through getting my tuck from there in breaks from school. They were used to children and were from London. They could quite easily differentiate from good and bad, and I was on their good list. I knew they would not embarrass me or ridicule me. Either they would or they would not.

They offered straight away without me giving any explanation and with no conditions. It was not a lot we needed, and I would never have taken advantage, but their kindness and integrity meant the world to me. I will never forget their generosity and compassion ever.

Some people without knowing, are angels.

After one visit to see my mam, the boyfriend offered to take me for a Kentucky but how could I indulge when I knew my younger brother was at home hungry. I refused on principle and even told him how I felt about my brother not having anything. He was completely undeterred by this and went and bought himself one anyway, which he proceeded to eat it in the car right next to me. I believe he took great satisfaction in it. I just sat there beside him, urging him to choke on it.

Even though I was dying inside for that Kentucky, the resentment I already had for him inside had increased tenfold. I felt pure loathing for him and just could not understand how a grown man could be so cruel and heartless. He wanted us to suffer and him trying to manipulate me made me so resolute in my determination to not show him one ounce of emotion.

He did not realise that at my grand old age of 15, I was way cleverer than the big red-faced lobster sat beside me scoffing his Kentucky, all greasy fingered and looking like a bit fat pig! He was abominable in every way possible.

I was learning very quickly that showing your cards would always leave you at a disadvantage somewhere down the line. I would always be loyal to my little brother. No matter what, my dear mam had ingrained that into me. I was not going to let this man have anything at all to use against me. I did not trust his intentions one tiny bit and I vowed there and then that I would never be anything like him to anyone in my life!

Up until now I had spent six years with this man in my life, but now, I was seeing his absolute true self. In all its glory, and this was just the tip of the iceberg!

I was desperately in need of women's things. I did not want to say to anything to my mam as not to worry her. I need not have worried though as unbeknown to me, she had been thinking the same. We had gone on a visit one day as per normal.

This day was different though. The boyfriend, my younger brother and I had gone in as usual. My mam was sat up, bright and beautiful as always. She hugged my brother and spent time talking with him.

If any of us, it was him that I felt for the most. He was the baby and she mollycoddled him completely. He hung on her every word and was a proper mummy's boy. Why would he not be? He was just 14 and she was his world. He may have only been a year younger than me, but I was very protective over him also. I was older than my years and always had been. Like my mam always said, I had been here before!

After a while of tending to my little brother and the boyfriend, she asked for time alone with me. Women's stuff she said. They left and my mam was on it. Are we eating ok, did I have deodorant and women's things? I was hesitant to say as I did not want to upset her, but she was adamant I tell her the truth (I didn't say about his Kentucky binges and the fact I was getting food on tick from the local shop), it just wasn't appropriate, and I knew it would have pierced her heart to the core. She knew what she needed to know. I was to be given the family allowance book to make sure me and my little brother had something to fall back on. When she explained to the boyfriend he was like, "Yes sure of course."

When we walked out of the visit, and all stepped into the lift he looked to me and said "I don't know where the family allowance book is though" with the most twisted smirk on his face. I did not say a thing, my stomach twisted in knots. I just raised my eyebrows and gave him a; 'I know you are lying look,' but I knew there and then that he was gunning for me. In his tiny mind, I had exposed him in front of my mam for the pig he was, but she knew anyway. He did not give a toss for us.

He showed nothing but contempt towards us but had still been cashing in on our family allowance and keeping all the money to himself. In the car on the way home, I acted as normal as I could and even made small talk. My little brother was oblivious. I was one step ahead of the arrogant fool and little did he know that I was going home to ring my NANNY!

All of my family were down in the six hours it made to take that journey, Leeds to Devon. Early hours of the morning they were there. The boyfriend did not know what had hit him.

It would take a lot for me to bring in the Calvary, but I knew when I had to. I always knew when I was out of my depth, and they knew it too.

He woke up to a very full house and they wanted answers. He found the family allowance book just like that. My family would have never shouted or screamed at him. Their presence was enough to make anyone quiver in their boots.

He was a spineless coward. The can of worms was opened now, and he knew it. He had always seen my family at their best and we all had the best manners and knew how to conduct ourselves when necessary. Our natural ethic was to help anyone in need and look after the neediest and weakest. I really believe he had all my family down as nothing but scum who had nothing. Materially we did not have a thing but in reality, we all had integrity, honesty, sincerity and love in bounds.

He possessed none of these!

My dear mam was unaware to all of this going on or maybe she was not. She was the cleverest out of all of us. She bloody knew everything and knew how to work everything. It must have been debilitating for her to say the least. All she could do was rely on the integrity of others, but the one person who she should have been able to rely on the most was not participating.

He was not able to accept it wasn t just about him and quite obviously was affected and hurting more than anyone else. There was enough pain to be distributed around for everyone.

There was enough sadness, anguish, guilt and heartbreak going on for the whole of the town to have a turn but unfortunately you can t change a person, only they can do that for themselves and whilst he was hurting so badly, he assumed everyone should hurt a bit more too. He was never going to make it easy for us!

My mams health was deteriorating rapidly and she was not feeling very good at all. She had developed pneumonia, as her immune system had taken a bad hit from the radiotherapy. There was a lot of talk going on whether or not to instigate the chemo. It was not to be so.

My mams immune system had so swiftly declined that any introversion into her system would kill her. The only hope now was that she would recover but the doctors had by then established their diagnosis.

There was nothing more they could do. We had to prepare ourselves now for her to die, my mam had not long left to live, a matter of weeks if that. There was no hope now, this was it, divine intervention was not even an option no more for me. The sheer magnitude of the prospect without her, left my whole being utterly destitute. How was I going to live without her?

It was then, that I caved in. I went out with friends and got absolutely smashed out of my head. It is like I wasn t consciously aware of what I was doing, but I had gone into complete self-destruct mode. I wanted to die too! I had people telling me she would get better and that everything would be okay!

I had just been told that day that she was dying and there was nothing anyone could do. We are talking about people around my age with all good intentions. How could they comprehend such a thing, they could not and up until the day before I believed all that too!

I understand that these people were just trying to be kind, but I just wanted to smash their heads in. I would not say my mam was dying for the fun of it. I was never an attention seeker like that. I was always a person of my word. I told the truth and did not contemplate ulterior motives. They were however my age but had not experienced anything that my life had, and I would often have to remind myself of that.

My family were up and down from Leeds like a yo-yo. Everybody wanted to spend as much time as they could with my beloved mam. I just could not handle she was dying. I did not want to accept it. It became harder for me to see her. I just could not look at her the same.

One day the phone rang at home, and I picked it up. It was my mam. I blurted out that no one was home, and she told me she knew this, and it was me that she wanted to talk to. I had not been to see her for a few days. I was awkward and felt uncomfortable, but she told me that she had missed me.

I was so missed by her and how much she loved me. She never once made me feel guilty, but I just could not find the words to tell her I loved her, I wanted to, so much, but I also knew it was also saying goodbye and I just wasn't ready for that!

I Just put the phone down feeling embarrassed. My mam never told us that she loved us, maybe it was a northern thing, it just was not something that was said. I always felt loved, it was not that, but we just weren't a lovey dovey family and I knew her saying that to me meant that the end was nigh!

I also though, felt like a right idiot. It was not about me; it was about her, and I knew then that I had to pull myself together. We did not have long, and I got myself together and went down to see her later that day, but I was not prepared for the sight that met my eyes.

I walked into her room. The change in her was drastic, she looked frail and older than her years and I just burst out crying. It was not like me to be so unguarded, but the shock literally knocked me sideways. My mam though was on it snappy, she told me that she was not haven't any of it and to leave and only come back when I had a smile on my face.

I was flabbergasted; I mean she was dying, how she could be so nonchalant about it. It was beyond my comprehension! I wanted to absolve myself in the whole misgiving of the devastating and abysmal circumstance it entailed. I wanted my moment!! I left the room, and my eldest aunty was waiting for me.

She explained that my mam did not want tears and sadness around her, and I had to get my head around it. My mam needed me to be strong for her. My mam did not and could not tolerate seeing her children hurting. I was crying

hard, and she held me for a while and after I had composed myself, she was like 'right head up girl, get in there and light up her world."
I did just that and my mam squeezed my hand as tightly as she could." That's my girl" she said to me with the most beautiful smile and the love that shone out of her will be etched in my memory for eternity. I immediately felt proud and accomplished. I was on her train of thought, and I would not let her down.

She was however becoming increasingly weaker by the day and on one of these days I was to visit her with my little brother. A nurse had come to check on my mam and to ensure she was comfortable, which was regulatory and of standard procedure.

The nurse poured my mam a glass of water and went to help my mam to drink it. My mam though did not want me and my brother to see anyone help her and asked the nurse if she could pour the water into a plastic tumbler so she could drink it by herself. The nurse did this and intuitively I knew where my mam was going with it.

My mam drank the water by herself, whilst shaking but the composure and defiance she did it with filled me with such pride, it must have sapped so much of her energy, but she was so determined, she then insisted on going unaided to the toilet.

The nurse stood and let her do it and by this time herself was choking up. It was obvious by then what my mam was up to, she was giving my brother and I a lesson and a big one at that. She made her way back onto the bed and winked at my brother and me and the love that radiated within that room was extraordinary.

The nurse told my aunty later, she had never come across a woman as strong and dignified as my mam ever and she was at the end of her nursing career to retire the following week!

She was dying but my mam was not going to give up without a fight and anyone forbid her children witnessing death in a morbid, morose or melodramatic kind of way.

She was braver and tougher than any boxing heavyweight champion I had ever known.
Mike Tyson was the man then. He had nothing on my mam!

I know you now.
You are the light the moon and the stars,
The spectacular sun that illuminates my sky,
The glistening dew that quenches my thirst,
The song that I sing, you are the verse.
You are Elvish honey, the Koh-I-Noor,
You are the eighth wonder of the world.
You are love, music, sunsets and laughter.
You are my everything.
My happy ever after.

THIRTEEN

TIME TO SAY GOODBYE

My family had made it clear that I was still a young girl and encouraged me to spend time with my friends. I was not to be burdened and even though I felt like I never wanted to leave my mams side, they were right.

I would still have my nights out down the under eighteens revenues, and back then there was quite a few. There was a big group of us, and we all got on great. The usual trials and tribulations occurred but overall, we were a good bunch.

It was around this time I started to become close to a new friend. We were quite a pair. I was petite and she was tall, five foot and eight inches tall, very tall and gangly. I was like a little terrier, where she was so placid and laid back. Our humour was the same though and she liked the laughs. She knew she would get them from me.

She had been trying for a while to befriend me. One dinnertime, at school, when I was sat on my own (because I wanted to be on my own), she casually walked over and asked if she could sit with me. The thing is she abbreviated my name (trying to be cool) and I particularly detested that abbreviation.

I looked at her with my deadpan, straight hard face and told her no, she couldn't sit with me. Then I told her exactly what my name was, in no uncertain terms. She just accepted it graciously and nonchalantly walked away. She was completely undeterred, and I liked that, she made me laugh inside. I had never seen someone so unoffended in all my life. She had balls! I knew I liked her there and then, and it wasn't long before I granted her my friendship. We complemented each other perfectly. She was to become a best, best friend of mine and until this day, still is.

It was one of my nights out that I'd had far too many to drink. I came back to the house and was being incredibly careful not to wake anyone up. I did not want anyone to know that I had been drinking. I took myself off to bed to be awoken early in the morning by the phone ringing repeatedly. I tried to ignore it as I was feeling a little tender, but suddenly it occurred to me that no one else was answering it either. I ran downstairs and picked up the phone.

It was my eldest aunty. As far as I knew my family were all back in Leeds at this time. My aunty was at the hospital. She was ringing to tell me that my mam had taken a turn for the worst, and I had to get there. It was not imminent, she was in a comfortable way, but it was just in case (It was in fact, brutally, imminent as fuck). My aunty was being considerate. My family had all travelled down through the night.

My aunty offered to come and collect me, I loved her for that. My aunty showed me what a beautiful person she was. If I had of said yes, she would have been there in the minutes it would have taken her to get to me, and it would have been minutes. Every red light would have been non consequential to her, every single thing that got in her way would have been stampeded and obliterated to oblivion.

My eldest aunty was a very powerful women, like no other woman I have ever met in my life, and I never will. I would not do that her. No way! I know in these times with my mam, she learned a hell of a lot about me, as I did her.

The journey to the hospital took forever but I did not mind. I was trying to protect myself from the whole nightmare. My nerves were another thing altogether though. I was physically trying to stop myself from shaking and it was not the last night's alcohol taking effect. I was nervous and did not like the tension and not knowing of what was to behold me. I knew it was not going to be a pretty sight. My mam had taken a turn for the worst; she was not that great the last time I had seen her, a worst sight was unfolding in my mind's eye, and I was preparing myself for the unimaginable.

I arrived at the hospital to be met by my eldest aunty. She had taken on the role of being the head of the family and she was doing an unfaltering job at it. She explained that my mam was totally unrecognisable to any thoughts I had of her and that I did not have to go in and see her if I didn't want to, but I had to though.

She walked me into the room and stood right beside me. I took one look at my mams face and everything I had imagined became blurry. I had no preparation for the sight in front of me.

It was horrific, and it was my mam! She looked like a zombie sitting up with her eyes rolling to the back of her head, she was foaming at the mouth, and I just turned on my heels and ran.

I did not know where I was running to, but I ran and ran and ran. My eldest brother, who had been working away in London but had been called home, was the one to run after me. He grabbed me when he eventually caught up with me and squeezed his arms around me. I was so angry and sobbing uncontrollably. He was crying too, but he had to give me a talking to. I will never forget how brave he was.

He told me that as much as it was soul destroying, I had to get a grip. He always had a way of making me feel safe. He said we would get through it together and I did not have to be afraid as he would always be there for me, if not in person, then in each other's hearts. He gave me courage when I needed it the most and a light when everything around us was so dark. I told him I would be there for him too!

We hugged hard and my big brother made me laugh so brazenly, because of our snotty faces, he mimicked us both crying and blubbering. I was in hysterics, and he loved my laugh. He was crying laughing; we were the worst for laughing together and my mam would have loved every single second it! My heart literally burst with pride then.

Even though we were dealing with the most heart-rending situation, my big brother was still able to put me before him. That was the ultimate testament to my mam. We were such a close family and for my brother who was only nineteen to show such courage, wisdom and above all love, made me feel so special and grateful. We would always have each other.

Right there and then I did not feel as alone as I thought I was.

My sister was working in London and the boyfriend had not thought it yet necessary to let her know. My aunties were absolutely livid about this. He had made out he did not have an address for her (she was a being a nannie to someone's kids). They knew it was his way of being spiteful. He particularly detested my sister, and out of all of us, he would have taken great glee her in her not having the chance to say goodbye to her beloved mam.

It is incomprehensible that a person could be so hateful, but I assure you this was the person he was. My aunties managed to get word to my sister, and she came back that day.

All these malicious things the boyfriend was doing were manifesting inside of us all, but energy had to be spent on my mam and not on him. I just hurt so bad for my sister; it was completely deliberate of him. If my mam had of died and my sister had not have got to see her beforehand, he would have relished in that.

My mam had been given a week at the most to live and we were to prepare ourselves. She had not spoken for at least five days by now and we all knew it was devastatingly imminent.

She though, had other ideas!!

By now, my whole family had taken over the waiting room. The nurses at the hospital were exceptional and just let us get on with it. We would in turn all sit with her, holding her hand whilst talking of our funny memories, the best memories.

It had to be happy of course, for when you are with a person who has a set certain precedent; you could not have been any other way. There were sixteen of us in total, not including the boyfriend. We would use our house as a base and go back to wash and change.

One morning, maybe six days later, a nurse had gone into check on my mam, and was utterly astounded as to what she saw. She came running into the waiting room stating my mam was sat up in bed! My eldest aunty went with her to take a look.

My mam, up until this point, had been literally on deaths door and could not communicate in any way at all. This was just too much to take in. That nurse must have mixed up somewhere along the line, but with that my aunty came back out and was grinning from ear to ear.

My mam somehow had come back from the brink of death to say her goodbyes!

This next bit is told in my mam 's words to the best account I can give:

She had been sleeping and an angel had come to her and told her it was her time to go. She had pleaded with him that she needed more time with her babies and needed to speak with them for one last time. It was a beautiful room they were in, white and light.

He had said to her it was her time to go, and that he would guide her. She said it was uniquely beautiful but all she could think of was her children. She had asked him for a little more time with her babies and the angel gave it to her.

My mam was sat up in bed talking as fluently and as effortlessly as the most abled person I had ever seen. It was astonishing, and she was making the most of it. Everybody was given a proper good talking to.

I was called in with my eldest brother. He was first. She told him how proud he made her and what a gorgeous, good son he was. He would always be her blue-eyed boy. He was her eldest and for that he would always be special. Those two had an amazing bond and he was always so respectful and gallant towards her. There was a lot more said but that was between them.

My turn came. My mam told me about me. She told me that she was proud of us all, but I was the one. I did not like that and became irritated. My brother told me to stop and listen. She said to me that I was special and that my brother also understood this. She told me I would blossom into the most beautiful little thing and had to be careful because men would gravitate towards me. This made me feel uncomfortable as I was not interested in that yet. She told me I would be successful and to watch out for jealousy.

All this she was telling me was making me feel awkward. She told me to never change. I was a beautiful soul just like my brother, sitting on the opposite side. She told me to be strong; Her body was just a shell and that her soul would never leave this earth. She loved us so much and her not being here would never change anything. The love she had for us was eternal and forever.

She squeezed my hand so tight; I felt her love and words surging through my body like dynamite had erupted through each and every vein. Every single part of my body triumphed and chorused with gratitude. Spontaneously my heart filled with limitless pride.

It was empowering and humbling both at the same time. When I walked out of that room I felt ten feet tall and in mighty awe of my incredible mam. She was nothing short of remarkable and I walked away from her that day feeling like I was prepared for my life without her.

My mam had done what she needed to do. Everybody had their talks and the feeling amongst us all was of positivity and virtue. We were all still living in the waiting room and my mam had concocted a plan. She was so weak by now but had coerced the nurses to wheelchair her into the waiting room. Much to our surprise, in she came.

My mam still had unfinished business. At the time there was a well-known song 'The only way is up," and she started to sing it! All of my family sat in the waiting room singing it with her. We were all singing at the top of our voices, full of victory and joy.

I encapsulated that moment in my mind and in my heart. It is one the best memories I have of my entire life. My mam was leaving us all, but she was leaving us with strength and above all, love. She showed everyone that day how it was supposed to be done. Well, she certainly showed me.

She was just the most selfless person in the world. My whole family loved and adored her and completely surrounded her. My mam emulated strength and dignity in abundance and still in her last days everyone wanted to be around her. She was magnetic and addictive; for a woman who had literally been at deaths door five or so days earlier, she was simply astonishing. You just cannot teach that to someone.

Everything she did in her final months was about everyone else. She made sure my self-worth was to be unreachable; a thing that no amount of money could buy. That no matter what life threw at me from there on by, I would be able to cope. She gave me the truth and told me to live by the truth.

She taught me always to do the right thing (even when nobody was looking). She taught me that I could live without her and that I had to live without her. She taught me to be a good person and never to compromise my morals. She taught me that no matter what, as long as I held onto my self-worth, I would always love myself, because without her here nobody else could love me like she did. She taught me how to be strong and she taught me well.

My mam passed the baton onto me and I in turn would pass that baton to whoever needed it. Something inside me changed that day and I completely felt the shift. She was ready to go, and I was ready for her to go. I felt different; she had done her job and she had done it above and beyond exceptional!

The following evening, I had a much-needed night out with my friends. I was staying at the house of another good friend of mine. The next morning, we were awake early, messing around and just having a laugh. She lived in a flat which was at the top of the building and her bedroom was extremely near to her front door. There was a knock at the front door and my friend's mam answered it. She came and told me the boyfriend's brother was at the door. I got out of bed and went to the door.

He told me my mam had passed away at 1.20 in the morning. He was so sorry, and he had come to take me home. It will be forever ingrained in my mind.

My friend's mam grabbed me and hugged me and burst into tears and my friend was just stood there with tears streaming down her face. My heart went out to them. They looked so hurt and pained. It was my mam that had died. All I felt was numb. It was the most bizarre feeling in the world.

The boyfriend's brother said he would wait outside in the car. I got dressed quickly; went out to the car. No words were exchanged on that journey home between the boyfriends brother and I. He was different to the boyfriend. I found him decent.

I was completely shattered and heartbroken. No words could express how I was feeling. It was final. That was it.
I would never see her face again.
I would never feel her touch again.
I would never hear her laugh again.
I would never be the same again.

All I wanted was to get home and see my nanny!

Fifteen years old and all on my own.

Even though I am surrounded I feel so alone.

My mother, my angel, has gone to the sky.

I will be strong because she told me to,

But I just want to cry.

Thirty nine years was not long for this earth.

But God seemed to see her undeniable worth.

I am blessed she was my mam.

She was amazing and strong.

But the road ahead will be painful and long.

I will make her so proud of me.

I will honour her name.

Her life on this planet,

Will not be in vain.

My beautiful mother,

My angel above,

I will love you for forever,

My cherished love.

FOURTEEN

THE AFTERMATH

My nanny was sat at the table in our kitchen when I walked into my house, exactly where I predicted her to be. She held out her hand and I walked over and took hold of it. I hugged her so tightly for what felt like an eternity. She was completely bereft and the change in her was like something I had never seen before. I could see right there and then that a huge part of her soul had departed.

It defied the lifecycle that my mam had left the earth before her, and she was only sixty-six years old. You are meant to go before your children. My heart broke for her. She had lost a child. My mam was only thirty-nine. My nanny had lost her beautiful daughter and I had lost my beautiful mam.

I felt her grief in an incredible abundance, as she did mine. I held her face and she held mine, in the cusps of each others hands, we did not say a word, what could have been said. Absolutely nothing. The unbearable was being shared between us. It was unspeakable!

We eventually spoke and agreed that at least my mam was out of pain and could be with the angels. My eldest brother came into the kitchen, and we all hugged each other for what seemed like hours. It seemed we were all on the same page, that in a way it was a relief as we did not have to see her in pain anymore.

It had to be the worst part in all of it. You can keep laughing and upholding the positivity but seeing the most special person in your life suffer, is an immeasurable suffering to oneself. We did not have to see her in pain anymore.

The suffering though, was to dwell deep inside of us all, for a very long time.

The rest of the family started to dwindle in and we all comforted one another with hugs and moral support. My youngest brother hid himself away, he was inconsolable. I was the one to go and comfort him and give him a pep talk. I told him that we had to pull together now, we had to be strong for our mam, we had to do her proud. It seemed to work.

I cannot make you get well.

I cannot make you okay.

I will just sit here and watch you fade away.

I am hopeless, I am unforgiving,

Of my uselessness.

I am drowning in this travesty,

All I want is for you to stay.

I am powerless

I am empty.

I have nothing left to give.

Where is God now?

Why doesn't he let you live.

My nanny somehow, got hold of my dad to let him know. We had not seen him in for a few years by then. He had cut himself off as he could not cope. Nobody knew where he was living or of his whereabouts. He must have made it clear to certain connections that he did not want to be contacted either. His name was mud.

My nanny and my aunties were not going to give up and eventually someone caved in and gave them his contact details. Me being me, felt no anger towards him. I had already grieved for him. My nanny was so angry. So were my aunties. They made it very clear to him that he had a moral obligation of some sort towards it.

He had no idea that my mam had been ill, so it was a hell of a shock for him. His hands were tied though; there was nothing he could do. He had a lot of resentment towards the boyfriend and his pride played a big factor in his actions over the years. He could not bear to see his children around another man. My brothers and sister held a grudge towards him because of it. I understood this completely, but I also understood him.

I hated all the animosity being thrown around. I did not want him near me if he felt cajoled and forced into it. Yes, he should know, but really what the fuck could he do? The estrangement from him had done so much damage already and to throw him into the mix, was just adding to the whole shit show saga!

The intensity of her dying had been so overwhelming and emotionally draining. It is so hard to watch someone you love dying and being completely powerless to do anything about it. It consumes your whole being.
My mam had died all by herself with not one member of the family by her side. That absolutely crushed me; all sorts went through my mind, had she been scared, did she ask for anyone?

My nanny though explained that my mam chose to do it that way. There was hardly a minute when she was not on her own. The nurses said she had passed over peacefully so that eased my conscience slightly. The guilt I felt was colossal. I should have told her I loved her.

There was a time in the hospital when my younger brother had come to me and was so overwhelmed. He wanted to tell my mam he loved her but there was always someone in the room with her. He just wanted his moment with her. Her baby son.

I told him to go into that room and ask everybody firmly to leave so he could have a few minutes with his mam, alone. Every person in the room honoured it and I knew they would. I gave him the courage to do that. He did it and afterwards he was a completely different person, he felt elated and accomplished and he owned it. He told me in precise detail what he did.

He told me so proudly how he walked in the room and respectfully asked everyone to leave as he wanted some privacy with his mam, and they all did. He told me how he sat with her and held her hand; how he told her how much he loved her, and she squeezed his hand as tightly as she could.

He knew then that she knew, she made him know with her last bit of might that he would know. It was so powerful for him, and I was so proud of him, and I hugged him and let him release every little bit of emotion. That moment meant everything to me.

For most of our lives I had been his voice, but I knew that this time it had to all come from him. I look back to that young girl and I am so proud of her. My brother came to me and opened his heart. It will never leave me nor him. I knew that day that our bond was unbreakable. I would never let him down and vice versa. Respect came from him to me that day.

The dog was suffering. It may seem a strange thing to add but over the years I have listened to many people state that animals have no feelings. If they had seen the transition in the dog from before and after my mam, they would have changed their opinions.

Literally his whole demeanour changed. He was an extremely confident dog before but now he actually looked bereft. He would barely get out of his basket and went completely off his food. He lost weight and was physically pining for my mam. It was so wretched to witness. I spent a lot of time cuddling him, he meant the world to me. He understood exactly what I was going through, I know he did! He always knew.

Still, things had to get sorted and the boyfriend had decided it was his way or the highway. I mean, he was paying for the cost of the funeral and all the arrangements so there was no way he was going to let anyone else have a say. Not even us kids. He was the most heartless, selfish bastard I had ever met!

Of course, the tension was brewing in a great, big pot, bubbling up so intensely. It was on its way to detonating an atomic explosion of grief. By this time, the elders wanted to kill him. They were in between not wanting to make it any harder for us kids and ripping his throat out.

My eldest aunty was one very tough woman, not a lot of men would have messed with her. She was very well respected in Leeds; all my family were. It was amazing to see her remaining calm. She was handling it with dignity and so much composure, even though it was twisting her insides out. The focus was getting us kids sorted.

By this time, I think everyone had been to see my mam in the chapel of rest. I had decided I did not want to go, and so had my eldest aunty. One day she and I were off to the next town where the chapel of rest was situated. We were going to buy my outfit for the funeral.

We were in her car with her reggae music blaring out. She really was the coolest aunty, with a head full of dreadlocks and a beautiful face, she was a perfect picture. She had to be the funniest woman I have ever known. I had grown up with reggae music and loved it.

We arrived at some traffic lights that turned left to the chapel of rest and all of a sudden, the music just stopped, we looked at each other, and both simultaneously heard my mams voice! It was such a vivid moment and surreal to say the least. We knew there and then that we had to go and see her. She told us there and then, that we had to.

When we walked in, I was completely struck by the size of the coffin. It was tiny, my mam was tiny, she really was so tiny, that floored me. My mam was massive in her stature. My aunty did not mess with my mam, and nobody would dare to cross my aunty. My mam was way much bigger than that coffin.

There was a man stood there. I asked him if my mam was in there and he just nodded. I walked over and looked at her and I told him straight away, they had put too much blusher on her cheeks, and she would not have liked that, so I asked him to tone it down. I ïm sure that 's why she intervened and made sure we went to see her!

My mam knew how to look good (she was vein) and there was no way she would have wanted to look like Aunt Sally! He nodded and said he would and I thanked him and told him not to forget. Other than that, she looked so peaceful and serene. I did not touch her though, I knew that was just her shell, for she had told me that.

My aunty had her time with her. It hit her hard. When we came out of there, my aunty held onto the wall outside and literally broke her heart. She sobbed loudly and unashamedly. She let every emotion go. I witnessed and felt privileged to see her grace towards my mam.

We were both at peace. Her big sister, my mam, gave us that last-minute decision to go and see her, and that for me, that was another very special bonding moment for my aunty and me. My mam was still letting us know she was around!

The boyfriend had been staying with a friend whilst my family were down. He was not doing it to be chivalrous; he couldn t stand being around my family. Anyway, it suited everyone better that way. My eldest aunty was consumed with hatred for the boyfriend. She had witnessed him do things whilst in hospital.

One of the things was chucking peanuts in the air and catching them in his mouth, whilst sat on the chair by my mams bed. My mam was terribly ill, and it was as if he was bored and wanted her to get on with it. For her to just kick the bucket.

On another occasion, he told my mam it was fine for her to let go, he was getting impatient it seemed. She attacked him for that apparently. She knew exactly what he was doing. I didn t want to hear those things, I didn t want to believe those things. How could someone who was meant to love someone (that someone being my mam) be so cold and callous. I couldn t deal with it at all. I didn t want to deal with it.

You see, unbeknown to me, when they had sold the previous house there was as a lot of money involved. He had made my mam believe it would be a wise decision for him to look after it. My mam was not driven about money and as much as she liked a nice house, she wasn t money orientated. She would have given her last penny to someone in need. Of course, he knew this! So, he had every penny in his name and money was his God! My family could see all of this and wanted us kids to have our share.

To be honest, I 'd had enough, and I couldn t have cared less. It was all beginning to get on my nerves. I just wanted everyone to be nice. I was sick of hearing about money and what was rightfully ours. ʻFuck money 1 thought, why can t everyone just be nice.

The day of the funeral arrived. It was nerve racking. I had never been to a funeral before and now I was going to my mams. I hated the cars picking us up outside my house. I found it cringe- worthy. All the curtains twitching away, and some people had the audacity to come out of their houses to watch us get into the car. I mean, talk about morbid curiosity.

To me, those people had no shame or integrity. I felt like running over and punching each of their ugly faces in the head. I hated being the talk of gossip mongering but I suppose those people did it because it gave them something to talk about. Many people thrive on the misery of others.

We certainly did not give them the show they wanted. Each of us retained our dignity and composure. My eldest brother and I got into a fit of giggles in the car and my sister was not at all impressed and told us to show some respect. We adhered to her warning but knew we couldn t look at each other then, or else we would have elapsed into hysterics.

We all had our way of coping and I know my mam would have been laughing with us. When we were looking at everyone 's sad, sorrowful faces full of pity, it evoked something inside of us. My brother and I found it hysterical. It was deviating us away from how we should of actually have really been feeling. We didn t want to feel that though. We simply could not deal with that feeling.

I do not remember much about the service, only that I didn t recognise a lot of people and I had stop myself from laughing at their pathetic, crying faces. It was just me, I always had to find a way to laugh, it felt much better than being sad. It was like my brain was trying to divert away from what was actually happening. I did not shed a tear. In the car on the way up to the cemetery, my eldest brother and I got the giggles again. It did not go down well. It was an absolute quagmire of conflicting emotions. But again, it was all nerves.

There was a huge turnout for my mam 's burial, which did not surprise anyone. She was a popular woman. I do not know anyone who could have disliked her. I know this made me feel good inside as she deserved the best sendoff; my very brave, beautiful mam.

I remember when they started lowering the coffin into the ground, the boyfriend went to put his arm around me. My eldest brother pulled me out of the way and put his arm around me instead. He was giving the boyfriend a clear message.

The boyfriend was crying and snotting all over the place. My aunties were adamant they were crocodile tears and that he could have won an Oscar for his performance that day!

Deep inside of me, I was inclined to agree.

Afterwards there was a gathering back at our house for close family and friends; you could not have cut the atmosphere with a hedge trimmer. My eldest aunty just stared daggers at the boyfriend the whole time, all my family did. He was not fazed though, as he knew it was not long before they would all be on their way home and he would have all the money to himself.

My youngest brother had decided to go back to Leeds to live with the rest of my family and so he left with them. Not before my eldest aunty spoke with the boyfriend though. I am not really sure what was said but he looked terrified. I know she wanted some money from him to kit my little brother out with new clothes etc. He offered her twenty pounds. Seriously! That man had no moral conscience whatsoever.

That was the straw that broke the camel's back, and my aunty apparently let rip. I am not surprised he was terrified. She was clever, and had in effect, put the fear into him. He was not so cocky anymore. It was gut wrenching saying goodbye to my little brother. I just felt that we needed to stay together. We held onto each other for a very long time, but I had firmly made my mind up that I wanted to stay and be with my friends.

My eldest brother went back to work in London and my sister went to work in a live-in position in a hotel. I was left with the boyfriend, but I knew I could handle him and just tried my best to stay out of his way.

Out of all of us I was his favourite. I was good at school and in general, I was easy. I knew he would be ok with me, and in many ways, I also mothered him to a degree. I also felt that if he were here to stay then we had to get on with it. In a way, he was the last bit of normality I had left.

He had also made a promise to my mam that he would always do well by us, take care of us.

He was to break that promise in less than a year!

You cannot condone your immorality.

Its wrath will not betray you.

It will seek you and confound your soul.

To impending, imperious loneliness,

Residing everlasting in your whole.

The truth will always be perilous within its fight.

For whatever is done in the dark,

Will be revealed in the light.

FIFTEEN

THE BETRAYAL

It is when it hit me the hardest, after my family returned to Leeds. The longing for my mam was like hell in my heart. It was a constant pining, a withdrawal symptom. Nothing had a purpose, and I was in a million tiny pieces trying to stick them all back together again.

My exterior remained flawless and faultlessly intact though. I would never crumble in front of anyone. My mam would not have tolerated that, I suppose that is what kept me going, trying to think what she would have said to me and how she would have handled things.

My mam, like she said in the hospital, was always going to be with me and she was right to a degree. She was still in my head and my heart at most times, but the lack of her physical presence was something I had to learn to live without, and it was crippling. The craving for her being was crucifying me.

Whilst my siblings and the rest of my family were around, there was always a distraction, someone to engage and have a laugh with.

The silence was deafening.

The boyfriend's sense of humour was pretty non-existent, and he was entirely immersed in his own self- suffering. I do believe in his own way, that he had loved my mam, but it was only to ever suit himself. I tried to avoid him as much as possible. He was never nasty to me because for one, I think he actually liked me, and he also knew my family were always at hand. He was obviously lonely, and every now and then he would want some acknowledgment about his status.

He told me one time of how I reminded him so much of her. I instantly felt uneasy. We were passing on the stairs. He stopped me to tell me that. I realised he was just trying to be kind to me, and nothing more. I thanked him, but even so, it made me feel uncomfortable. It would have been a welcome compliment from anyone else, but I didn't like it coming from him at all. I think I was actually quite motherly towards him and in some ways, I looked at him as a child. I suppose I felt that adults are meant to make you feel safe, but I just didn't feel safe with him.

At times if I were home on my own in the evening, I would sit downstairs. Every now and then, he would come home and sit on the armchair, we would make small talk and he would just start bawling his eyes out. I would comfort him from afar with the odd word of sympathy, then I would politely make my way up to bed, hearing him wailing and crying. I would lie there thinking "shut the fuck up."

On one occasion, I ventured back downstairs and told him blatantly to "fucking stop it." He did right away and apologised. I just walked back upstairs thinking it was a good job he did, or I would have punched him one. I felt it was all over dramatic, like he was over embellishing it, it felt strangely odd. He was lonely and he missed her so much, but it was more mechanical, like a performance of some sort. I just could not put my finger on what was going on.

He would go out for walks at random times. Sometimes it would be raining, but then he would come back bone dry. He was acting suspiciously. He never got one show of emotion from me though. I just did not trust him at all. I wanted to keep an eye on him.

I was never going to go back to Leeds. Life up there was fast paced, and everyone fended for themselves, as my younger brother had started to find out. He was becoming homesick, and I started to have a little butterfly floating around inside my tummy. He was coming back. It was too much for him to deal with.

He had been used to one to one when my mam was alive, and she was always compassionate to his needs. I think my family made it clear that they did not have time to mother him. That wasn't in a bad way either, he just had to get on with it, but he was left feeling bewildered and lost.

My nanny would drink most nights, and not just a couple of glasses of wine. She liked her whisky and strong lager. This was not anything new; she had been doing it all our lives and wasn't about to change now.

I know it was one of the reasons why my mam had left Leeds in the first place. She could not cope with all the shenanigans and dramas and wanted to minimise our exposure to it all.

My nanny didn't have the emotional capacity to cater for my brother. He wore his heart on his sleeve and whilst he was craving affection of some sort, she was not the person who could give it to him. Her way was the hard way. "Fuck love, get money" was her motto.

Life had made her extremely bitter before loosing my mam. Her bitterness had now become so much more rottener and putrider. She had no friends and sat at her round kitchen table every single day, without leaving her house.

My little brother was coming home! I was so excited and could not wait to have him back. We hugged and cried; we were so happy to be back together again. It became apparent now though, just how much the whole saga had affected him. He was quiet and insular; the hurt was unmistakable through the bleakness in his eyes.

He was also quietly festering an unrepentant anger inside. It had really taken its toll on him and I, being me, did not like to see this. He would always open up to me though, and now I had him back I was going to look after him.

The boyfriend in his insatiable, attention-seeking self, had no time whatsoever for my brother. He was jealous to death of the attention my mam gave him. He had been brought up army-style all his life and thought my little brother needed this kind of influence in his life also. On a couple of occasions, he had tried to man my brother up, whilst my mam was alive. The boyfriend was not scared of spiders and had taken it on himself one cold morning to go into the shed and catch the biggest spider. He then proceeded to make his way to my brother's bedroom and throw the spider on him whilst shouting 'Surprise." My little brother shrieked so loud and was utterly petrified, as you could imagine!

My mam had jumped out of bed like we all had. I had run out of my room and was disgusted; I shouted to him that he was a 'fucking sick bastard." My mam went to punch him, and he ran out of the house. The fucking army upbringing had done him no good, so why would a seemingly intelligent person want to inflict his own insecurities on a vulnerable 13-year-old child.

Later that day whilst my mam and I were doing the dishes, we were discussing his antics. I was telling her how she did not need another baby as she already had us four, I was sympathetic and asked her why she was with him; what we didn't realise is that he had decided to return home with a big bunch of flowers for my mam (nothing for my brother though) and he had heard our conversation!

He stormed through the door with the flowers in his hand and threw them on the floor, whilst declaring how he had just listened to our whole conversation. My mam and I stood staring at him with our mouths agape. My mam (who was washing the dishes), picked a plate up and threw it at him; he turned like a flash and legged it out of the house for the second time that day!

My mam answered my question; she did not know and didn't even think she loved him anymore! It beggars belief till this day what an absolute arsehole he was.

It was around this time that the dog died. I was absolutely beside myself. Apparently, he had chased a car and was run over! (As my eldest had said once before, he finally became Sam spread!). That dog was my world. He comforted me like no other person could, I just adored him.

It was like the end of my world, and I was devastated. I was so angry, and nobody understood. I believe, in hindsight, it was the catalyst of my understanding of death.

I was not ready to accept my mam was dead. (It was too much for a young mind to comprehend), but I could somehow deal with the death of my dog. I cried an ocean of tears for him. I was heartbroken. I was also extremely suspicious of the boyfriend; he had loved that dog also and I wondered if he had faked his death, especially more so when the boyfriends' true intentions unfolded!

With my brother coming home, the boyfriend had installed a lock on his bedroom door. He also had a lock on one the kitchen units to keep HIS goodies in there. We were used to him and because we had the Calvary in Leeds, he was tip toeing around us. We were ever respectful because we knew inadvertently, we needed him.

Instinct is a virtuous beholding; I was lucky to possess it and I was truly thankful for it. I knew something was going on, but I had no idea what. I was soon to found out though and again, it was another drop kick right into my little heart.

I had come home from being out with my friends. Back then mobile phones were just a thought in another person's mind who was a twinkle in their dad's eye; we were not able to communicate instantly like nowadays. If you wanted to get hold of someone, it would be either through word of mouth or ringing another person's landline and back in 1990, not everyone was privileged enough to even have a landline I arrived home and there was my little brother looking so forlorn and worried.

It turns out the not-so-clever boyfriend had left the padlock open on his bedroom door and my brother had gone in for a snoop. He had found letters between the boyfriend and the neighbour to our right. My brother was crestfallen as he explained the content. The boyfriend and she had been having an affair (hence the random walks and coming home bone dry when it had been raining). What really did it for my brother though (and me), was how we were described.

She wrote of how she could not wait for them to buy their house together and leave us four horrible fucking bastards behind. I had read enough (whilst in front of my brother). I gave him a hug and told him it would all be ok. I made doubly sure there was no evidence that the letters had been seen and I also had a read for myself.

It made me feel sick. It took every last bit of restraint that I had, to not go round to her house and annihilate her. I knew, I would have fucking ripped her to shreds. My energy was not deserving of her.

She was the most grotesque, ugliest thing I had ever seen. Her nose was literally bigger than her entire face, she was vulgar too. The way she treated her children was despicable. Her husband did everything for those children (he was a good man, her husband, and I liked him). She was known to be the old bike; anyone could ride her. She was vile and overall, an absolute waste of oxygen. So, we were the fucking bastards?

My brother and I went into the boyfriend's bedroom to make sure everything was right back in its place, just as he had left it. He, after all this time, did not quite realise, we were just as crafty and as a snidier as he was. I then opened up his wardrobe and there was nothing in it, his drawers were empty too. In fact, all of his belongings were gone apart from the one thing that had exposed him, his upmost personal things, including the letters from the big fat buffoon next door and all his precious memorabilia.

He must have been a day away from absconding.

The boyfriend came home later that day completely unaware that his plan had been exposed. He walked in so normal. He had no idea. I asked to speak to him upstairs. I had told my brother to stay put. I am not going to lie, I was shaking in my boots, but yet again my mams words resonated around my head. He looked perplexed and was all in a complete kerfuffle. I was straight to the point! We had found the letters, and I knew that he was about to leave!

He burst out crying. He just could not handle it, he was sorry. Nobody understood him and it was the worst thing he had ever been through in his life. He just could not face it and it was so terrible for him. I told him I could not find it in my heart to console him. I told him to look at me straight in the face. I told him I was a sixteen-year-old girl who was stood before a man who had made a promise to my mam. He just broke down and was at my feet begging for forgiveness. I can honestly say I was repulsed by him.

I did not feel an ounce of sympathy for him. I would have respected him if he told me straight that he could not handle it, but he was looking to a kid to resolve his conscience, to unburden him. He did not get the reaction he thought he was going to get.

I asked him how he felt, crying to a sixteen-year-old girl and asking her for forgiveness. I told him how it made me feel when I read those letters. I told him straight to the point what an absolute coward he was. Then I told him to leave, but not before telling him that he should be ashamed of himself.

Why he just could not have been honest. My naivety did not understand why he could not be honest. Money, that's what!

That day I knew I had become a woman way before my years, and I knew then, I could take on anything or anyone. The truth always prevails in the end. My younger brother was beside himself and was fretting over the fact we now had no guardian. He was perfectly justified in worrying and I told him so and hugged him tight; even though the boyfriend was utterly useless, he was still keeping a roof over our heads.

I was on the phone to my brother in London immediately; he was not due home until the weekend, and he told me to ring Nanny! Again, my whole family travelled down through the night and, as you can imagine, were furious. My eldest brother could not rest and came home as well.

The situation was serious, and a solution was needed quickly. Emotions were flying high! I just felt empty. Hadn t we been through enough already? Why was this happening to us? We were just four children; who were simply grieving for our mam.

The boyfriend though, was not resting either. He had left his beloved stereo behind amongst other precious memorabilia of his. My family had realised this and were confident the weasel would be in touch. To think if my younger brother had never found those letters, he would have certainly done a moonlight flit!

My mam was still working her wonders.

My family had a plan; we had to reel him in. They suspected he would call (and because I was his favourite), I would speak to him. I knew I had to do it and play the game as it was the only way. They were right. He called, and after two days of being on phone duty, it was a relief. I was shaking from head to toe, as I was so angry with him. I really never wanted to see him again. I just was sick of it all. I just wanted peace, and in my head, I just thought 'let him go.''

All my family were stood around and the tension was so dense it felt tangible. Firstly, he asked if I was ok, and he made general small talk, then he went for it. Could he come and collect his stereo and all of his other personal belongings. I had been told to say yes on the condition he brought all of mams personal belongings back.

Her jewellery he had taken (and all of it) and everything else he had wrongfully taken. He thought about it, but the stuff he still had left in the house was of much more importance to him. He agreed. I told him all we wanted was to remain on good terms, and that there was no bad feelings. He could come and collect his stuff at the weekend.

He was such an immoral man that he turned up as planned. I let him in and was dismissed from the room. He had, in effect, entered the Lion 's den.

He came with some of my mam's things, but not all of them. My eldest brother did all the talking. I was stood behind the door, knees knocking and absolutely petrified at the prospect of what could happen.

My brother (in a metaphorical term) went for the boyfriend's jugular. Where was my mams money? There was not any left, the boyfriend claimed. My brother knew there was, but the boyfriend was crying again. He had not given back all my mams precious belongings either, he was insisting on having his things and leaving. My brother had enough.

After a long pause I heard a roar. At the top of his voice, he shouted to the boyfriend to get out of the fucking house before he fucking killed him. The boyfriend ran as fast as his legs could carry him, empty handed and screaming "HELP" as loudly as he could, whilst running out of the house. He then proceeded to report my brother to the police!

The police turned up at our house with a job to do. There were four of them. To their credit, by the account the boyfriend had given them, they must have thought my brother was an axe murderer in the making. They banged on our door like they were about to enter into a crazy, mental asylum. I answered, crying and shaking, and I could see their resolves weaken instantly. It took seconds for them to assess the situation.

They took statements from everyone in the house and there were a lot of us. By the end of it, they were just flabbergasted. The policeman that took my statement had to excuse himself for a minute. His tears were visible as he did so.

Each and every one of those coppers shook my brother's hand as they left and told him to enjoy that stereo. Yes, the boyfriend had really only rang them, to retrieve his precious fucking stereo!!!

There is to be no winners in his game.

Everyone has lost.

But whilst dignity has been retained by most,

One being, has been left with a cost.

A burden the soul cannot carry lightly.

Will seep into his veins.

And pump through them nightly

It will devour his whole.

And be in embedded into his mind.

It will be moulded into his callous heart.

And never peace, will he find.

SIXTEEN

THE OUTCOME

My family were desperate for my younger brother and me to return to Leeds with them. As much as my love for them was of a greater magnitude than any love I had for my home, I was still resolute in staying put. I felt safe there; even though everything around me was bedlam, I could not bear to be away from my mams life and her memory. It was a comfort for me to have her all around me; I kept everything as I possibly could, to her high standard.

She would laugh at me when she was alive, as she would leave chores for me to do, like the dusting for instance. I would casually flip the duster over and move a few ornaments around to make it look convincing, but she would leave traps! She knew me so well. She would say "right madam, get that duster and do it properly."

She made me clean around my bedroom window with a toothbrush once as there was mouldy condensation. I was absolutely incensed by it, and she knew it. It was her way of showing me that no job was beneath me, and it is exactly how I clean now. She made me clean the fridge another time, but it was not just a wipe out, oh no, I had to get in all the creases and crevices and get the real congealed residue out.

She only ever made me do those jobs once, but they have never left me. Our microwave was spotless inside, like new; everything was. If any of us had a bath, it had to be cleaned afterwards and woe betide if she would find a dirty ring around it. She would always know who the culprit was, even if she was not home.

My little brother got off with mostly everything, she would make it clear that he was just the baby and I accepted that without giving it a thought. We would all tease him "Aw Mammy's little baby" and he would relish in it; you could just see how special it made him feel. He was pardoned from any chores at all.

If you were going to do any job, it had to be done thoroughly. I just thought she was bloody mad, wasting her time cleaning like she did, but anything my mam ever did, was always done to the highest degree.

She would never cut corners, and one of her favourite sayings was "Never put off until tomorrow what you can do today."

There is a photo of her and my eldest aunty, with my mam holding a cleaning cloth. It was completely staged, and I look at that photo now with so much adoration.

My mam kept everyone and everything in check. She would take no disrespect from any of us, and we in turn, were taught to respect each other. If she heard one of us even call the other a pig or a cow, she would go ballistic. She would not tolerate nastiness, bitchiness, slyness or manipulation at all, and she would only let the teasing go on for a short while before she would intervene.

She kept a very close eye on our manners and the truth, and I mean, the real truth, which was what she expected. She would never let any of us get away with anything, and we would always pay a consequence for our misdemeanours. Whether it be not being allowed out for a week or getting banned from using the phone. She would never, ever relent.

I was never scared or frightened of my mam though. She was mostly warm and tactile; and could make me feel like I was the most special person on the planet, but she had boundaries and for the most part I respected them.

I was in my bedroom one day after school and my younger brother had come home. He did not know anyone was home and I heard him shout "Mam, I'm home." I became rigid to the root. He then shouted it again. I made my way down the stairs and approached him as attentively as I could. He looked crushed when he saw me, and I sat down beside him. I asked him if he was ok. He just burst into tears.

He told me that he just wanted to come in and say the words he had always said when he came home. He never wanted to stop using her name. I knew exactly how he felt, and I know she would have loved that. I just loved him all the more at that moment. I hugged him and told him that I completely understood, and that he should never stop doing it.

My little brother was heartbroken. He was her baby, and he was totally lost without her. He was the one I really had to keep a close eye on and I did.

The social services became involved, and it was just another thing to think about in an extremely, uneasy time for us all. My younger brother was only fifteen, and as much as I thought I was a woman, I was just sixteen and had no idea of how the big world really operated. A meeting was arranged at the house with a social worker. I cannot tell you who was there that day; all I knew was that these people, this social worker, were there to determine mine and my little brother's future.

My big brother however, had already decided we were all going to stay in that house and stay together. He would make sure everything was taken care of. He was a mere 20 years old and that was a huge decision for any man to make, let alone a very young one at that. He was my hero, and I was so thankful to him, but my heart hurt so bad for him.

He told her in no uncertain terms that we were not going anywhere and that she was wasting her time. He was so sure of himself. There was no room for negotiation. We had all been through too much already. We were staying together, full stop. I felt in awe of him right there and then, and so incredibly grateful.

The meeting was to go in our favour. She was a lovely woman and so compassionate. I think she had seen that we had been through enough, and our mental well-being was of a huge consequence to her. As much as we appeared strong and durable, she could obviously see how vulnerable and fragile we all were, it was her job to do so. She would have to make the case heard in front of a panel of people from some sort of higher establishment, but she was positive it would be the same outcome. I felt reassured by her. I believed her and was right to do so.

They let us be and the relief was immense. The uncertainty of what could have been, was causing turmoil inside my head, and now, that was gone I could rest a little. My big brother was working and was being paid a decent wage. The overheads on the council house were minimal, so financially it was affordable.

By now, I had a little job in a bakery and was earning money of my own; my brother had made it very clear to me that if I needed anything, then I had to ask him, but I just couldn t do that. He knew this, so he would ask my friends what clothes I liked and buy them for me, or he would tell me we were going into town and would make me buy things. I did not want to put on him at all, but inside I was so proud of him, and I knew my mam would be too. He was just so virtuous and brave; the love and respect that I had for him, was absolutely immeasurable.

We had a plan in action, and for the first time in a very long while, I started to unwind a fraction. It was all very scary and uncertain, but we could only give it a go. Most importantly, I was starting to feel secure again.

The boyfriend 's actions had left a lasting impact and were continuing to do so. It transpired he had not been paying the bills, and the final demands had started landing on the doormat, equating to a considerable amount of money. Outstanding to pay was around eight hundred pounds, which of course was a lot of money, and just another kick in the teeth. My poor big brother was at his wits end and not surprisingly so. It was just one knock after another.

My mam would have been turning in her grave, this would have been her worst nightmare; she did not deserve the insult to her memory, and more importantly, the boyfriend knew how much our welfare was to her. The only thing she asked of him, was that he take care of us kids. 'Take care of the kids."

With everything going on, my brothers, my sister and I, didn t even know that my mams headstone had been erected. None of my family were told first. We were told by a family friend, who was hurting to tell us. They just said 'I am so sorry, but you need to go and see".

I went straight away. I ran the mile and a half, it took to get to the cemetery, in what felt like minutes, and it probably was minutes. My P.E teachers at school would have been in awe of me (I hated P.E).

I arrived at the cemetery and knew exactly where her grave was, even though I had only ever been there on the day of her burial. I felt proud of myself for that. I was atrocious with directions usually, my mam was with me, I knew that!

Her name and the date she had died had been inscribed and the words, 'Into the sunshine of God's love" then followed by just the boyfriend's name.

Into the sunshine of god's love….the boyfriends name.
Into the sunshine of god's love…..the boyfriends name.
Into the sunshine of god's love…….the boyfriends name.
Into the sunshine of god's love…………………………………

I did not only re-read those words four times. I inhaled, absorbed, swallowed, encumbered, and compartmentalised those words. Then I re-read those words a million times and more. I just couldn t believe that he didn t put our names on my mams gravestone. I really just couldn t believe it. All the things my Nanny and aunties had said about him were true. All of the times I wanted everyone to be nice. All the times I wanted everyone to shut the fuck up and just be nice. All those fucking times.

Those words that he put on my mams grave were imprinted so affirmatively in my minds eye. No insult would ever hurt me. I became bulletproof then.

I knew then, I knew who he really was. When I read those words, he started a war with me. A silent war, a very silent, guarded war. A war, that would take planning. A war that in time, would become so ferocious and loud, the whole world would know about this war.
A war that I would win.

Sing your sweet victory.

And bloody sing it loud.

Be the big man you are.

I hope you are proud.

It really was the final nail in the coffin. After everything he had done to us already, and after everything we had been through. He would probably never visit her grave. Everything he ever did had an ulterior motive. He was a callous, vindictive bully, who was just full of pure venom and greed. I knew one thing; he would never win at whatever sinister game he was playing. I pitied him immensely, I really did.

The others hated him and were to store it away for later years. I decided to forgive him. I did not like to hold onto resentment, but I would never forget. As my eldest brother would say, I had the memory of an elephant. It was beyond comprehension what he had done to us, but even then I believed he would have it all paid back to him, in some form or another. Karma being one!

My dad had decided it was time to make an appearance. We had been talking since my mam had died. He had made it clear that he would not come anywhere near, whilst the boyfriend had been on the scene. It caused friction between us all. I think I was deemed as quite naive, as it seemed from other perspectives that I would forgive anyone for their mistakes, but I knew different. I could always understand everyone's point of view.

My dad, when he was younger, was extremely volatile. He would act with his fists at the slightest injustice. It may have been that way then, but by now he had remarried, and his wife was of a nervous disposition. She had given him a focus to remain calm and in control, for he would have hated to upset her in any way. He had stopped drinking in pubs years beforehand and avoided arseholes like the plague.

He knew we were not being treated fairly over the years and quite frankly, he wanted to kill the boyfriend. My dad knew his capabilities and his weaknesses and had to make the decisions he did based on these assumptions

Of course, when you are a child, you do not understand these things. Ultimately, my siblings felt rejected, and they were perfectly in their right to feel that way.

The night before he was due to arrive, I did not sleep a wink. It was the first time I did not just feel heartache! Excitement was prevailing, and I felt

deliriously happy, for the first time in a very long time. I was going to be reunited with my dear dad again.

It was like we had never been apart. The bond my dad and I shared was unbreakable. I just wanted to spend every minute I could with him. I had to start work at 6.00am and he would get up every morning to take me.

We talked about everything, and I opened up to my dad about the years without him. He was honest to me about everything, and he made it clear that my mam was the love of his life. I told him that whilst she was very poorly, she had asked for him. He was so choked, and we hugged for a long time. It was effortless between us because all I had ever felt about my dad was love. He wanted to try and be in our lives again, but the resentment from the others was overwhelming.

My younger brother got absolutely obliterated on the drink one night, and was totally pissed, he had been out with his mates and had made his way home. He was rolling around in the back garden shouting every obscenity under the sun at my dad. He was angry at my dad for abandoning him and wanted him to know about it.

My loyalties were to be with my brother, and I told my dad so. My dad had a taste of his actions thrown back in his face and even though I understood why he did what he did; my brother did not and was showing him exactly how he felt.

I calmed my brother down and got him to bed, but the whole episode impacted hugely on my dad. It was then that he realised he should have and could have done more! My little brother was not showing his true feelings, of course. He was hurting, and as any of us knows; when the drink is in, the wits out. I still laugh at the whole saga now though. My younger brother never did anything by halves, and I loved him for it.

My eldest brother had accepted my dad was coming to stay but decided to stay in London, he was also resentful towards my dad, but for much different reasons. He was the man of the house now. Why did my dad think he could turn up for us all suddenly and start to play happy families?

My dad stayed for two weeks and realised a lot of damage had been done which was way beyond repair. I had the best two weeks with him and enjoyed every single second he was around. He tried, maybe years too late, but to me he tried, and I loved him all the more for it. His door would always be open and for me that was enough.

It was now well established that we were on our own. A choice we all made. My family in Leeds were just a phone call away and would be with us anytime in the six hours it would take the journey in a car. I would speak to my nanny at least twice a week and my aunties would ring at least once a week to check on us all.

I absolutely adored my family for their love for us and their impounding determination to ensure our stability and reassurance. When you have this enforcement and sanctuary to fall back on, it replenishes your confidence continually.

My heart may have been shattered, but between them all, they were trying endlessly, between themselves, to put it back together, whilst their world had also been rocked from pillar to post. My mam was after all, the glue that held everyone together. It would bring the most tragic of circumstances to be encountered down the line though.

I would still ring my dad also. I was working full time and had a fantastic social life. It was just the way it was meant to be I suppose. There is no other way to try and evaluate it. All of us had to accept that my mam was gone, and she was never coming back.

I did not want to be angry and blame anyone. What was done was done, and it was just so painful that I had to find a way to make my life happy in one way or another. My mam told me that, and if she were here, she would have killed me if I had not have listened to her.

Everything was different now. My university dream was gone, and I knew I had to accept a different way of life now. I had to work, and I had to be strong, and I was beyond that. I did not want to talk about my mam to anyone and I was not going to let her death define me.

I was not a victim and I made sure I was not treated like one either. I felt so lucky that she was my mam. I was determined to honour her name. She was just so gracious right to the very end, and she packed a lifetime of wisdom into me. I was going to try my best not to let her down.

Everything I did in those first couple of years was for her. I thought about what she would say and how she would have dealt with it, and I would usually come up with the right solution.

I was plagued by the fact I never told her that I loved her, and that she died on her own; with not one her beloved family beside her, and even though I believed what my nanny had told me, I was angry with my mam.

Eventually she came to me in the most vivid of dreams about a year after she had died.

There was a welcome home party for her at Wembley stadium. My brothers and sister were there amongst so many other people. I was so vexed that she felt she just come back like that, after dying and devastating us all. I was trying my hardest to avoid her. My eldest brother came and told me she wanted to speak with me, and in his usual calm, but stern manner told me to go and see her. There was so many people surrounding her, but he told me exactly where she would be. Up on the highest stall in the stadium.

I wouldn t disobey my brother, so off I reluctantly went to find her, and there she was. Just her, in her favourite dress that we had buried her in, looking absolutely, radiantly beautiful. She told me she understood why I was angry, but it was so very important to speak with me.

She told me she had come back for me, she had to tell me that she knew how much that I loved her, and it was just so powerful and so real. She wrapped me in her arms, and I finally felt free. Free from the wretched burden of guilt, that had so mercilessly being anchoring my heart and weighing me down. Then, just like that, she was gone.

I woke up and looked straight at my alarm clock, it was twenty past one in the morning, the exact same time that she had died. It was incredible. Immediately, my conscience was as clear as it had ever been. Everything I felt in the dream, I felt it awake.

My mam was still taking care of me and guiding me. Death was not going to prevent her from being my mam.

It was time for me to start living again.

The tears fall in my alone time.

And I look to the sky for answers.

Hoping and praying that somehow, she can hear me.

I will endeavour to do my best.

I will honour her sincerely.

I long for her touch, her gentle words of wisdom,

The smell of her cooking,

Her voice of reason.

She has not left me though,

I still feel her with me,

She has not left me.

She is just sleeping.

SUMMARY

There is a gaping hole somewhere inside that no one else can see. It permeates your heart and soul, and some way or somehow it must be filled. Losing a parent at any age is utterly staggering and damaging to a person's wellbeing; however, the lifecycle is inevitable and at some stage, when a person has effectively flown the nest and created their own life, it becomes part of the life process.

The impact of grief, trauma or any hardship will affect every individual entirely differently, and it will affect us all until the day we die. There is no guidebook to refer to, and it can be despairingly lonely and tremendously daunting.

Grief engulfs us with multifarious emotions and as a teenager, I had very little life experience into the intricacies of those feelings and how to try and manage them. I knew though, that I didn't want to feel bitter, and that somehow, I had to get better.

When dealing with such a traumatic circumstance, the trivial everyday moans and groans pale completely into insignificance. In some ways, it catapulted me way ahead of my years and for many years to come I felt extremely isolated and lonely, even though it would have never appeared so.

There was a huge sense of rejection and abandonment involved for me, as even though my mam had died, I felt deserted and rejected. She was the only person that truly loved and wanted me, and I knew that no one else could ever love that me that way.

I was never jealous of seeing my friends with their mams, in fact it warmed my heart, but it made me feel like I was a freak of nature, ostracised, an outcast if you like. I was deemed different then; for some people it defined who I was (the girl that lost her mam) and I despised it.

The void my mams death left was unexplainable to anyone and probably more so because I knew they would never be able to comprehend the sheer enormity of the circumstance. I never spoke to anyone about it and if anyone tried to broach it with me, I would just shut them down without any negotiation.

It was way too private and painful. I would deal with what I had to in my alone time and usually in the dark of the night, and as quietly as possible. It was way too deep for me to expose, and I never wanted anyone to feel awkward around me. I always hated seeing people uneasy in any situation and there was something in me that liked to make everyone feel good.

I just couldn t put on anyone and quite frankly, there was not a single thing any person could have done to help. How could anyone mend my broken heart?

I could only try and fix that for myself and that is what I was determined to do.

The hardest thing of all was seeing the damaging effects it had on my brothers, sister and the rest of my family. Her death unleashed a catalyst of so much anger, bitterness, resentment and sadness; it was utterly devastating and unbearable to witness at times.

I just knew I had to remain as strong and composed as I could. I could always hear my mam telling me to do so. Her death later on, was to generate a tsunami of events that was to leave a trail of so much more devastation for us all down the line.

My friends have been invaluable to me, and I have chosen the best that is for sure. Laughter has been the antidote and probably the most significant thing of all that has enabled me to cope. No matter what, I have always been able to laugh; again, my mam taught me that.

There are certain adults I encountered in the very early years after my mams death, who showed me love and quietly supported me.

My manager at the bakery in my first job, who just understood me from the get-go. She had a knowing and understanding of life and just took me under her wing.

I took an order on one occasion for an 18th birthday cake and when the lady came to collect it, she started shouting at me that it was wrong, and she was going to ruin my life. To be honest I found it quite amusing, and, in my mind, I was thinking that I had her address, and that I would ruin her life. She then demanded to speak my manager.

With that, my manager appeared and as cool as cucumber, asked her what the problem was. The woman started to shout her problem and my manager went and found the book to check the order. I had written that she wanted a round cake instead of a square cake. I don t think I had ever got anything wrong before that, my manager knew I was a good worker. To keep the peace, she offered the cake for nothing (this is what I believe the woman wanted all along, a freebie) but the woman still wasn t happy and nastily declared that she was cursing me and my 18th birthday and wishing something terrible to happen to me. With that, my managers whole demeanour transformed.

Her tone of voice altered from passiveness to extreme assertiveness, and she told the woman to stop right there. She told the woman that I, as a 15-year-

old girl had already been through more that than that despicable w
have ever imagined and returned the curse back to her.

She then proceeded to order her off the premises and told her tha
wouldn t be having any cake at all. The woman didn t even try to a
she was way out of her depth. I was just completely in awe of how
majestically she conducted the dignified, barbaric slaying. It remin
my mam and that really meant something special to me.

The woman shrivelled into her shell and turned swiftly on her hee
simply left. My manager and I both cracked up laughing. She looke
without any obligation and I respected her ultimately. That job was
meant to be at that time because that lady looked after me in so man
without her even knowing.

My best friend 's parents who took me to Butlins were again, just wha
needed in my life, and again just at the right time. They were norther
called a spade a spade. Whilst at Butlins my friend and I got caught u
group of lads and we 're have a blast. Just flirting and banter but we d
realise the time. It was around two in the morning.

We quietly tiptoed into the chalet to be greeted by her dad, who wer
ballistic on us. We were sent straight to bed. I liked that, it felt like ho
from home.

My friends mum told me years later that one day whilst making up o
at Butlins, she found a photo of my mam under my pillow. It totally cr
her; but she never treated me with kid gloves and I loved her for that. 1
treated me just as they did their daughter and, in their way, showed me
they cared.

I found out my friends older brother worked with my mam in a restau
He would go home telling tales about this funny Yorkshire woman. I lo
my mam made an impression on him.

Over the years, the chats I had, and still do with my friends mum, have
priceless to me. Her parents hold a very special place in my heart.

A lady that lived down the bottom of my road was an angel to me. She w
funny, kind and just treated me like I was part of her family. When I wen
my holiday to Butlins, she turned up at my house the day before with a ba
full of brand-new clothes for me, without making me feel embarrassed or
awkward in any way at all. She wasn t having me going away looking lik
tramp she said. She understood me and knew I was proud.

There were also people who turned their backs on us when my mam died.
People who appeased their consciences by telling themselves that there wa
nothing they could for us. People who whilst my mam was alive you woul

ve never believed it of them. They lost a lot of respect from my brothers, y sister and I. They lost out.

eath is the one and only certain thing in this life, it shows no mercy in age, lour, creed, the rich or the poor. It does not differentiate in any way at all. It not personal to the people left behind and that for me was the most valid ement of my understanding that enabled me to cope.

Acceptance was for me, my saviour. I understood that the day my mam ed, it was final, that it was her time, and that was just the way it was meant be. My mam told me all those things and watching her accept her fate, nabled me to accept mine.

learnt the most valuable lessons of my life surrounding my mams death, and or every ugly act I observed, it taught me exactly how not to behave.

t has been 35 years since she passed, and I can honestly say, without any question of doubt, that every single day she has been in my thoughts. Her guidance and advice, for the time she was with me, has made me the woman I m proud to be.

I feel ultimately fortunate I had a mam who fought for what she believed to be right. A mam who tried her best at giving us a good life and for putting us first. I know so many people who haven t had the privilege of that. It will always make me feel eternally grateful.

Love is the most powerful and humbling emotion of all. A manifestation of our surroundings. It is predominantly the most important ingredient of all, in order to help anyone or anything grow. Without love, we are fundamentally worthless. The love that was instilled in me was beyond priceless. I am asked at times how I am so strong. I know now, it is all because of love.

The lessons I have learned are invaluable to me and no amount of money could ever buy what I have been given. We are born into an illusion that money is power, and it most certainly is to a degree, but you simply cannot buy love, health or happiness and that for me is all I ever wanted and needed.

For many years, I never thought I would ever find true happiness, but I can finally say that I am happy now. Married to a lion heart of a man by name, and also by nature. A strong man, who 's morals, integrity, love and kindness match mine. A man who will fight to the death for what he believes to be right. A man who is wise and smart, not governed by anyone or anything, only what he believes to be right (and for the most part he is). The funniest man I have ever met and known, but woe betide the person who upsets the

ones he loves, be that at their peril. A man who lets me be the strong woman I am. A man who lets me be free and above all, a man that I respect.

I am so incredibly fortunate to have gained the most wonderful mother-in-law. A very beautiful, strong lady who supports me and inspires me in so many ways. No one could ever replace my mam, but the respect and love that I have for her, has instilled so much faith in me. A lady who understands me like no other as, for herself has been through extreme hardship; She wears hardship like the rich wear Vicuna.

I am, above all, blessed to be a mother. A decision I never took lightly, and for many years it was strictly off my agenda. They have given me the gift of what I, and my siblings gave to our mam.

Simple, unassuming, reciprocal love. They have given me a purpose and I would sacrifice my life for theirs undoubtedly so. It would destroy me if anyone were to hurt them. I understand so much more now.

My youngest aunty after a lot of blood, sweat, tears and frustration, managed to acquire the deeds to my mams grave. I admired her for that so much.

My youngest brother after a few years, had a plaque made with our names inscribed. He placed it over the boyfriend's name. Into the sunshine of god's love and our names, her beloved children.

When I look back on that fifteen year-old girl that was me, I want to envelope her as tightly as I can in my arms and tell her what an absolutely, amazing, wonderful, young girl she was and how her mam would be so very proud of her.

The words, I know, she so needed to hear.

If I could tell the world all about you,

I would write them a book,

So the world would know too.

How the thunder would cower,

How the lightning would dim,

How the wind and the rain,

Would calm at your whim,

How your presence was solitude,

Never granted or gained,

How your laughter and love,

Ceased much of the pained.

If I could tell the world all about you,

I would write them a book,

About supreme virtue,

I would honour your name,

So everyone would know,

Just how much you were loved,

And continue to be so,

How the names of your children,

Were left off your gravestone,

By a spineless cunt*   **For my nanny**

Praying now for a backbone.

If I could tell the world all about you,

I would write a book,

So the world would know too.

In loving memory of my beautiful mam.

Printed in Great Britain
by Amazon